'ONEY FOR JAM

Essential Guide to Starting
ur Own Small Food Business

SECOND EDITION

Oonagh Monahan

Published by Oak Tree Press, Cork, Ireland

www.oaktreepress.com / www.SuccessStore.com

© 2017 Oonagh Monahan

A catalogue record of this book is available from the British Library.

ISBN 978 1 78119 295 5 (paperback)
ISBN 978 1 78119 296 2 (ePub)
ISBN 978 1 78119 297 9 (Kindle)
ISBN 978 1 78119 298 6 (PDF)

Cover design: Kieran O'Connor Design
Cover illustration: lepas2004 / iStockPhoto.com
Author photo: Anna Quinn

CONTENTS

ACKNOWLEDGEMENTS

Since the first edition of *Money for Jam* was published, legislation has changed, new food trends have emerged, new food businesses have been established, and others sadly closed. The reaction to the book has been really positive and encouraging. Nascent and start-up food producers across the country have contacted me to say how helpful it has been to them, while many students of food business use it on their third-level courses.

The recent changes in the legislation – in labelling especially – prompted this new edition. I've also included some more information about food units that are available to rent, additional ingredients, packaging and equipment suppliers, new routes to market such as the Food Academy from SuperValu and Bord Bia, and emerging trends including plant-based foods.

Brexit notwithstanding, I've included information for food producers in Northern Ireland and the UK. I've expanded the range of competent authorities to include the Food Standards Agency and Food Standards Scotland, as even though the parting of ways might see a divergence of legislation down the road, it is likely to remain the same for the foreseeable future. Legislation aside, if you're a food producer in the UK or NI, then the Food Standards Agency or Food Standards Scotland is the place to start for information.

Thanks again to the producers who have allowed me to feature them again in this edition, and also to the new entrants: Marjorie O'Malley, Achill Island Sea Salt; John Brennan and Sean McGloin, Blake's Always Organic; Philip Martin, Blanco Niño; Breda Butler, Cuinneog; Danilo and Helen Dozio, Dozio's of Mayo; Michael

Kelleher, Goodness Grains Bakery; Angela Hession and staff, Hillcrest Foods; Pauline Clarke, KooKee; Linda McClean, Mallow Mia; Martin Hamilton, Mash Direct; Eilis Gough, Mileeven Fine Foods; Declan and Yvonne Rafferty, Rafferty's Fine Foods; David and Martina Burns, Richmount Cordial; Carolanne Rushe, Sweet Beat; Dearbhla Reynolds, The Cultured Club; Aisling and Michael Flanagan, Velvet Cloud; and Paul Phillips, West Cork Pies. Contact details for all the producers featured in the case studies throughout the book can be found in **Chapter 16**.

I am sorry to say that three of the people featured in case studies in the first edition are no more. It's always a pleasure meeting and working with food producers who work so hard and have such passion for the food business and such a shame when they have to close, whatever the reason may be.

I've continued to gather information from a variety of sources for this new edition. Thank you especially to Cian Condron of Teagasc, Fiona O'Loughlin of About Hygiene and Helen Nzekia of the Coeliac Society for their valuable help. If I have forgotten to acknowledge or thank anyone, please accept my apologies for the omission.

Finally, once again, thank you so much to my family, colleagues and friends for their support, patience and encouragement.

Oonagh Monahan
Alpha Omega Consultants
Dromahair, Co. Leitrim
June 2017

1

INTRODUCING THE OPPORTUNITY

Have you ever thought about trying to earn some money from producing food? Are you the person everyone goes to for their lemon meringue pies, apple tarts and other desserts for family occasions, celebrations or other events? Do you have a garden full of rhubarb or other fruit? Do you make jam every year and give it away when you could be selling it? Do you fancy the idea of making cheese or yogurt or ice cream? Or are you big into baking sourdough bread or making fermented foods and would like to turn your hobby into a business – but don't know where to start?

If so, then this is the book for you – it will tell you everything you need to know or show you where to find it for yourself. *Money for Jam* is structured and written in an easy-to-follow and easy-to-read format. It is not a textbook – think of it instead as your trusty companion, more of a handbook or manual. It aims to reassure both prospective and current early-stage food producers. So, don't be intimidated!

Money for Jam contains everything that someone who is new to the food business will need to get started and to keep going. It will help bread bakers, cake makers, jam and honey producers, ice cream, yogurt and cheese makers, sporty protein bar and energy ball producers, hummus, pesto and dips processors, chocolatiers, dessert makers and more!

It covers the what, where, who and how for small food producers – including legislation and registration, labelling and packaging, suppliers and distribution. This is the part that puts off most would-be food producers. The complaint I hear all the time is that people don't even know where to start or who to ask for information in relation to starting a food business. Many are afraid to stick their head above the parapet by asking the Environmental Health Officers (EHOs) at the Health Service Executive (HSE) in the Republic of Ireland or their local Council in Northern Ireland and the UK, the Department of Agriculture, Food and the Marine (DAFM), the Food Safety Authority of Ireland (FSAI), the Food Standards Agency (FSA), Food Standards Scotland (FSS), Bord Bia or the other agencies. There is a common perception that doing so may bring unwanted attention – or worse, inspection! But the various agencies are there both to protect the consumer and to help you as a producer.

Recent Trends

Keeping an eye on consumer trends is essential if you're thinking of starting up a new food business or developing new foods in an existing business. Among those that have really grown in popularity in recent years are fermented foods, like kimchi or sourdough bread; healthy, convenient foods; high protein foods, which were aimed at sports people initially but have become more mainstream; foods to eat on-the-go; foods made using traditional methods, like craft bread; vegan / plant-based foods; gourmet convenience, like flavoured salt and the huge variety of dips that are on the market; or cookie, cake and bread mixes.

People say they want simple food ... and simple food usually means meat, vegetables and soup, homemade and wholesome. However, consumers are still time-poor so simplicity, convenience and good nutritional credentials are important considerations.

The past 10 years have seen a huge change in the way people think about the food they eat. Gone are the days of limited choice, low quality and tradition. People are now used to having a wide choice. People talk about food in ways they never did before. Standards have increased and with them, so have people's expectations of quality, value and availability.

The average person now knows their organic from their locally-grown, and their air miles from their sustainable. Not alone that, but with cheap air travel and the range of other nationalities now living here in Ireland, the consumer is more open to trying out new foods. What was exotic some years ago is run of the mill now. For example, hummus has almost become a staple food in many people's weekly shopping – but my mother reckons she didn't taste broccoli until she was 30! It just goes to show you that the foods many of us consider to be part of our basic shopping basket today were considered exotic and unusual years ago. The same thing will happen in the future for foods that are considered exotic or unusual now.

Now, more than ever before, shoppers are really interested in knowing where the food products they purchase are made and who made them. In addition, consumers care about health and nutrition, ethics, quality, naturalness, craft, and story and heritage. So, their decision to buy a food more often than not will depend on whether that particular food addresses these concerns.

Some small shops have responded well to this demand for quality and choice from customers. A typical example is a small butcher in a country town, who might have sold bags of potatoes and some vegetables, might have had packets of spices on the counter, even might have offered the occasional home-baked apple tart. The same butcher has now re-branded from, say, 'Quinn's Butchers' to 'Quinn's Fine Foods and Delicatessen'. The shop has had a facelift, it's more attractive inside and the layout has been tidied up. It is still selling the same foods but it has raised the bar in terms of how the consumer sees it. As a result, it is attracting new customers, offering an outlet for and showing support to local producers, and demonstrating that it is on board with the whole 'foodie' culture that has grown in recent years.

Opportunities for Small Food Producers

But what does all this mean for you, the would-be food producer? Let's say you have been baking or pickling or making jam or whatever at home mostly as a hobby until now, and perhaps the pressure is on to make some money out of it either to add to the household income or with the ambition to grow it into a decent business that will earn you a living. If so, then you need to know what you have to do to turn that hobby into a business.

Many consumers like the idea of supporting their own. They want to see money staying in the country, preferably locally. So, locally-made produce is very much welcomed and can be seen in shops everywhere. And the more there are, the more that encourages others.

Consumers like the idea of artisan or home-made foods. You might portray the image of a country kitchen making scones and jam in a cottage with roses around the door, while all the time you're really in a state-of-the-art food production unit in your converted garage! While the reality might be less romantic as you outgrow your kitchen or small premises, it is important to maintain that brand image for your customers. We will look at branding later in **Chapter 6**.

Irish and British consumers are more discerning now than they used to be, they are used to having a wide selection of foods to choose from, they expect good quality, and they are used to paying a little more for it. Farmers' markets and country markets have become the norm for many shoppers, not just some quaint novelty. Consumers will still make a special trip for special purchases that they cannot get in supermarkets.

The Artisan Food Market

Artisan / speciality food production in Ireland and Britain is made up of a large number of small food producers. The sector comprises niche products generally made in small batches, using artisan techniques. Mintel has reported that the production of speciality food in Ireland accounts for approx. €700m *pa*, up from €500m in 2013, and growing, and this is from a base of at least 300 producers. Since then the number of small producers continues to grow. The Supervalu Food Academy alone has supported over 300 producers, many of these new since 2013.

The artisan / speciality food and drinks sector continues to grow in the UK also, where there are over 6,000 small producers, clearly making it a very important part of the food industry and of the economy there.

The key point is that, if your products are good quality, with a strong provenance, are consistent, have great taste and flavour and ideally provide something a little different, then there is probably a market for them.

What Does 'Artisan' or 'Traditional' or 'Farmhouse' Mean?

Over-use of these words in describing foods has confused consumers and diluted their true meaning. Descriptions including 'fresh', 'natural', 'artisan', 'farmhouse' and so on are used widely, and may not always be accurate.

For the consumer, the word 'artisan' or 'farmhouse' means a connection to the individual who makes the food. In the consumer's mind, this means literally home-made or hand-made. Both the FSAI and FSA have published some guidance on this, which you can find on their websites. For example, to be 'artisan', you must employ fewer than 10 people (including yourself) and produce less than 1,000 litres or 1,000kg per week, among some other considerations.

Consumers expect 'artisan' to mean superior taste, flavour, hand-made, small-scale, with a direct connection to the producer, high standards – and so more expensive? While consumers like the idea that someone has made this food themselves, that it's not from some big, faceless, corporate, automated process, the question is whether they are willing to pay for it? The difficulty faced by small food producers is that they are in competition with those very same big, faceless, corporate, automated processors that can make and sell their foods much more cheaply. It's not so much that artisan or craft foods are expensive; it's that other foods, because of mass production, have become relatively cheap.

So, the artisan producer has a job to do in promoting all the qualities of their foods that justify the price – back to flavour, quality, provenance, authenticity, person, home-made, farmhouse, local and so on. Those are your potential unique selling points (USPs) – more about them in **Chapter 2**. You must never underestimate their value or forget them.

'Local' Is Important

When you think about 'local', do you think about your corner shop, village, town, county, province or country? When is local not local?

For some people, local food means that it comes from literally a local farmer, butcher, baker or a neighbour, or certainly within a distance of

100km according to guidelines. Consumers say that they like to support local producers and to shop locally, but if your name or the name of your food or business does not immediately tell the shopper where the food is from or that it's made locally, then you need to make sure that you let them know some other way. You can use your labels and branding to help communicate this message – more about that later in **Chapter 6**, when we look at branding and marketing.

If someone goes to the trouble to look for locally-made food, then they usually have a good reason to do so. Most of the time they want to be sure that their food can be traced back to where it was made. The phrase 'farm to fork' is used commonly now, and it's all about traceability – knowing where food and its ingredients come from and giving the consumer trust.

When is Irish not Irish?

- If it's *made* in Ireland? Even if the company is not Irish-owned?
- If it's not made in Ireland, but the company is Irish-*owned*?
- If the basic ingredients are not grown in Ireland, yet the food is made here by an Irish company, such as chocolate or coffee?
- If the *name* implies that it's Irish?

Whatever the answer, there is a great opportunity for you to shout about the fact that your foods are made in Ireland, by you, in your kitchen, employing local staff (even if it is just you and your family), using Irish ingredients ... or a combination of some or all of these.

The Advantages for Small Food Businesses

The small food business has potential for several reasons:

- Consumers have an expectation of being offered a variety of foods;
- Consumers are willing and able to discern and to pay for high-quality locally-produced food;
- Increased education and awareness levels of farmers and producers;
- Increased popularity of locally-produced, artisan, home-made and farmhouse products;

- An image of Ireland as an unspoilt tourist destination that is green, natural and wholesome;
- Availability of high-quality and high-profile local cuisine in the form of well-known, local artisan food producers across the country, thus raising the profile for all producers;
- New routes to market available (**Chapter 6**).

As far as the shopper and consumer are concerned, the main advantages for them are that the food is locally-produced, that it has low food miles as well as a low carbon footprint perhaps, is available locally, that there is a story behind it that they can identify with (the 'provenance'), but most of all, that the food has superior quality and taste. It can have all the local, eco, history and whatever you're having yourself but, if it doesn't have great quality and taste, then no one will buy it again. This leads to a key point about developing your food idea – make sure you get the taste and quality right first before you start telling everyone how great it is!

Irish food has the reputation of having high standards, good quality and trustworthiness. Food producers and suppliers should never forget the value and importance of building their brand around the provenance of their produce. Consumers like the idea that the food they buy is artisan, home-made, almost as if it has been made for them especially. They like to hear about the producers themselves, the farm, the family, the recipe being handed down through generations, tradition, history of the herd or breed and so on. It helps the consumer to satisfy themselves that the food is local, has not been overly-processed and meets their expectations of taste and quality. So where to start?

2

WHERE TO START?

Don't be paralysed by fear! Starting your own small food business is not like splitting the atom or finding the cure for a terminal disease. It's just food. Plenty of other people are already doing it, so it cannot be that difficult – or can it?

Nonetheless, there are so many different things to consider when starting up a food business that it can seem overwhelming. How do you eat an elephant? One bite at a time. First things first, then.

What Will You Make?

Before you do anything else, you must make up your mind about what food you want to produce. Most small food producers get into the food business because they love making something in particular or they have a source of ingredients that they want to use, such as fruit, milk or seaweed. Others get into it because they see a business opportunity in a niche area. Many new producers try to do too many varieties too soon and become overwhelmed trying to manage them all. Some decide to produce foods that they really don't enjoy making but do so because they think there is a market. Others do not have the skills required to make the food they think they would like to sell.

It is best to go with your strengths. If you don't enjoy making it, you'll not stick at it. So, the first thing is to say to yourself that you are now in business, selling food for money. It may be just a few jars, loaves or tarts to begin with, even in just one shop or market. But take baby steps, and when your confidence builds, then start to walk with your foods to a few more shops ... jog to shops in the next town ... run, grow the business if that's what you want to do ... all in good time.

New producers get all excited about their venture, which is great. I love enthusiastic people. However, sometimes the excitement focuses on the fun stuff: branding, packaging design, thinking about growth in the future, nationwide sales ... before they ever develop their food. All brand and no product. So first, you have to make something, a bit of product development!

Where Do Ideas Come From?

For many people, getting into the small food business is a matter of looking differently at what they might be doing already. As I've said above, you might make desserts on request for family and friends already and now want to sell them ... to strangers. Perhaps it's a case of trying a new venture simply because you've always wanted to give it a try. Or maybe you've lost your job (or your spouse / partner has) and it's a case of having to do something to bring in some money.

Whatever the reason for it, now you need to get your thinking cap on and decide what it is that you want to produce:

- Have you spotted a gap in the market? *I can't get good gluten-free bread anywhere!*
- What are you good at? *People love my lemon meringue pie or brown bread!*
- Do you already have a source of ingredients? *We have loads of blackcurrants in the garden ... I could make jam, pies, sauce!*
- What are the market trends? *I need something healthy to eat on the go.*

Who Are Your Customers?

You will need to consider who will buy and eat your wonderful food – your 'target market'. Your potential customers fall into two groups – the general buying public (the consumer) and the retailers who will buy from you to sell on to *their* customers. Both groups look for the same things: quality, taste, value and something new.

Your target market is made up of consumers of different types. Think about who they may be: families, older people, children, single people, married couples, men, women, healthy eaters, dieters, indulgers, students or workers? Your target market will influence the size of portion you make: large or small, multi-pack or single pack? Your portion size in turn will influence your selling price.

Next, consider your packaging: pre-packed or unwrapped? If your food is aimed at the eat-on-the-go market, then portion size and packaging style both need to be considered. There is more about all of this in **Chapter 5** on Product Development.

Retailers are also your potential customers, since unless you can sell through them you may not reach the consumer at all. Many retailers are keen to promote Irish producers: they see the sense in offering consumers a choice, and promoting local producers is a way of bringing in more trade. What you must remember, though, is that the retailer will not want more of the same – so try to offer something different.

Who Are Your Competitors?

If you go into almost any small shop, there will be at least two varieties of most foods. Take apple tarts, for example – your competitor might be another home baker in the locality, or a large bakery delivering to the same shop, or the shop's own in-store bakery. Most shopkeepers like to offer their customers a choice, so they provide a range for the shopper to choose from. Competitors also include anyone selling rhubarb or other fruit tarts or desserts that might distract your potential buyer away from buying your apple tart. So, your competitors include other small and local food producers, as well as the large supermarket suppliers, the discount stores ... and the list goes on.

Before you say it, everybody is a competitor! Everyone and every product has a competitor, whether it is an obvious one or not. Realising and acknowledging that fact is really important when it comes to promoting and selling your food.

You should benchmark yourself and your food against your competitors. What are they doing well that you might emulate? Can you beat them at their own game? What can you offer that is better than the food that is available in the shops? What price are they selling at? What is their packaging like?

What Is a USP?

A Unique Selling Point (USP) is a characteristic or attribute that distinguishes your foods from your competitors. Identifying and promoting your food's USPs is an on-going task. You can't just mention them once and sit back waiting for either the customers or the money (or both) to pour in! You will need to remind your customers about them all the time.

Some examples of a USP include novel packaging, 'free-from', natural, no preservatives or additives, low-fat, home-made, locally-produced, organic, uses local ingredients, or a new type of food product, new to this country, new to this area, healthy, different portion sizes – you name it! Whatever your food's USPs are, you must be clear about them in your own head first, and then be able to articulate them, talk about them and promote them all the time.

A USP defines your food's competitive advantage. It is essential to identify what makes *Oonagh's Apple Pie* different from its competitors – on as many different fronts as you can.

Who Should You Talk to First?

If you go to the websites of the Food Safety Authority of Ireland (**www.fsai.ie**), the Food Standards Agency (**www.food.gov.uk**) or Food Standards Scotland (**www.foodstandards.gov.scot**), they will tell you that the first thing you should do is acquaint yourself with the relevant legislation. For most people, that's enough to send them running for the hills. Legislation? NO, thank you!

However, if you're in this game, then there is no avoiding the legislation. The important thing is to know what applies to you and what does not. There is the challenge – how do you find this out? And, once you know what applies to you, then how do you interpret it?

Depending on the foods you want to produce, then your kitchen might be either very straightforward to organise (bread, cakes, jam, dips) or might be more complicated (meat, dairy, prepared salads, large amounts of anything). If you are going to make anything at home, or even if you plan to convert your garage or move into a small premises, then the very first thing you must do is to phone your local Environmental Health Officer (EHO) at the HSE if you're in the Republic of Ireland or your Council for Northern Ireland or the UK. These are the people who will give you approval for producing most foods. Microbreweries also must register with the EHOs.

If you are planning to get into hen or duck egg production, or animal slaughter and handling and / or processing meat, or fish, or making dairy products, then in the Republic of Ireland you need to contact either the local DAFM office or the Sea Fisheries Protection Authority. In Northern Ireland or the UK, contact your Council, which also may inspect establishments involved in animal slaughter and handling and/or processing meat. So, check out your Council website or call them to find out who you need to talk to.

If you don't know who to call, just call one of them and they'll point you in the right direction. We will look in more detail in **Chapter 4** at food safety and hygiene.

Getting Organised

For the best chances of success, you will need to think through all of the issues that affect how you will make, where you will make and how you will package and label your food. In addition to your job as production manager, initially you also most likely will be the financial controller, sales and marketing manager, office manager and administrator, trainer, staff supervisor (if you have anyone working with you), delivery van driver, and chief bottle washer!

It is very difficult keeping on top of everything, of that there is no doubt. Your chances of success will improve if you at least know all the things you are supposed to remember. Make a list (keeping everything in your head is impossible) and if you can't do it all yourself, then get some help. There a useful Action Plan (if I may say so myself!) that you can download from my website **www.alphaomega.ie** to help you identify and remember everything you need to do.

Many people who have started up a small food business from home still try to maintain their 'other' jobs as housekeeper, parent, cleaner and cook. In my experience, women are particularly guilty of this. You need to acknowledge the fact that you have now set up a business. It might be at home but it is still a business. Schedule time for when you will be 'at work' and during that time, no other household chores should distract you. Easier said than done I know, but you must aspire to achieving that goal ultimately.

Common Reasons for Failure … and How to Avoid Them!

Food products fail all the time – usually for one or more of these reasons:

- **Poor market research among consumers or retailers or poor market orientation (in other words, trying to sell to the wrong people):** You think your product was great, your family and friends have told you so, and maybe it was. But none of the customers want it. Or you're not targeting the right customers, or there is already a well-established or even a better version already on the market and it is proving very difficult to convert shoppers to buying yours. Or perhaps you're trying to sell in the wrong kinds of shops;

- **Technical problems:** Product problems or defects in production. Perhaps making a few cakes in your kitchen was manageable, but once you start making 100 every week, you might find that it just cannot be done at home due to limitations with your mixer, oven, and/or refrigerator. Or, while your recipe worked well for a 6" cake, it didn't rise when you tried to scale it up for a 12" cake. In this case, you needed to do some recipe and method trials and tweaking (product development, in other words – see **Chapter 5**);

- **Insufficient marketing effort:** Making the assumption that the product will sell itself. One of the jobs that some food producers hate is having to get out there and sell. Most will be happiest in the kitchen, up to their arms in flour or sauce. However, if you won't or can't do it yourself, then get someone who will and who will do a good job representing you and your foods and will make sales. We will look at how best to approach this in **Chapter 6**;

- **Bad timing:** Nothing as obvious as trying to sell Christmas cakes in July, but perhaps the market wasn't ready for your chilli chocolate bars/low calorie stout/kidney bean brownies. Indeed, it may be something you could not have anticipated, such as a local factory closing down with job losses, the result being that people locally are not willing to spend money on perceived indulgences;

- **Higher costs than anticipated:** If sales and marketing is one bugbear, then financial planning and costs analysis is the other for most food producers. Nearly everyone hates looking at the figures but you must calculate how much it costs you to make, pack, distribute and sell the food. You must do this sooner rather than later. If you don't do it, then you cannot put a retail price on your products except by taking a wild guess. If at the end of the year, you have worked every hour of every day and sold hundreds of pots or pies but still have no money for shoes, then there is a problem. We will look at how best to approach this in **Chapter 8**.

In order to increase your chances of success, learn from the experience of others:

- Produce to consumer demand for the artisan / premium market;
- Get the training you need – don't presume you know it all;
- Develop online sales for foods that can be shipped easily;
- Promote your USPs and brand values – quality, flavour, taste, provenance;
- Build awareness about your brand and your food by telling people about them all the time – word of mouth, advertising, networking;
- Use your network of friends, neighbours, family and colleagues – it's great for spreading the word and for exchanging information;
- Develop new markets over time – always be on the lookout for opportunities, don't get complacent, you never know who will come in on your turf;
- Use social media!

- Keep your product range fresh by bringing in seasonal and occasional varieties, or by trying new packaging and labels.

In order to maximise your chances of success, control the things you can control. Find out the things you don't know, don't ignore them. Knowledge is power. After that, you are at the mercy of the marketplace, the economy, and the unknown unknowns!

Just Do It!

If you're not already paralysed by fear, then you might be overwhelmed at the thought of trying to manage everything. However, most people don't go from zero to huge volumes overnight. It is most likely that your success will grow slowly at a steady pace.

There is a bigger danger that you might plan and plan and plan, but never actually make anything. My advice is *Just Do It!* Get on with it! Make a couple of loaves / pots / jars / bags and get yourself down to your corner shop and see whether they'll take them from you for re-sale. What's the worst that can happen?

3

NAVIGATING THE FOOD SAFETY AND HYGIENE LEGISLATION MINEFIELD

Before you even begin to tackle food safety and food hygiene, let's take a look at who is responsible for food legislation and for monitoring that it's being done correctly.

The concern that people most often voice to me is that they are afraid that the authorities will either stop them from starting up at all or close them down and prevent them continuing. There is only one answer to that – you must make sure you keep your Environmental Health Officer (EHO) or Council or DAFM Inspector (if you are farm-based) on-side! The key to this is communication, so contact them sooner rather than later. They will visit your home kitchen or small unit and take a look at your set-up. They will tell you whether it is suitable or not (and you may be surprised to find that you have little or no work to do to get it up to scratch!). They will offer you great advice about what changes you might have to make.

Your EHO or Inspector is your best advisor – these are the people you must satisfy. And if you don't register with them (in other words, let them know you're in business), they will catch up with you eventually. Whether it's from spotting your foods for sale in shops, at markets or shows, seeing your adverts or just hearing about you, they will find you!

While all of this might sound a little frightening, be assured that the FSAI, FSA, DAFM, EHO or Council Food Inspectors are there to help you. So, who are they?

Competent Authorities

The legislation mentions 'Competent Authorities' a lot. These are the government agencies and departments that are responsible for writing and enforcing the food legislation. So, who are they?

- FSAI – Food Safety Authority of Ireland (Republic of Ireland);
- FSA – Food Standards Agency (Northern Ireland and England & Wales);
- Food Standards Scotland.

The Food Safety Authority of Ireland (FSAI) is the government-appointed authority dedicated to protecting public health and consumer interests in the area of food safety and hygiene. Its principal function is to take all reasonable steps to ensure that food produced, distributed or marketed in the Republic of Ireland meets the highest standards of food safety and hygiene reasonably available and to ensure that food complies with legal requirements, or where appropriate with recognised codes of good practice.

The FSAI is responsible for the enforcement of all food legislation in Ireland. It does this through the EHOs at the HSE, DAFM, County and City Councils, Sea Fisheries Protection Authority (SFPA) and other bodies. Which one of these applies to you and your food business depends entirely on what you are making:

- For most people producing small quantities of food at home, it's the EHOs. The EHOs' job is to ensure that food legislation is followed properly. They are also educators and advisors and they work very closely with the owners of food businesses to build compliance with the law. The EHO ensures that you, as a food producer, understand that there is a law, what your obligations are under that law and what the possible consequences might be if you do not comply;
- DAFM is responsible for anyone producing eggs, processing milk or making dairy products. Anyone who wishes to manufacture a dairy product or process milk for direct human consumption must contact the Dairy Hygiene Division within DAFM in the first instance. An information pack is issued to the potential producer,

outlining what is involved and covers requirements for both raw and pasteurised cows' milk, goats' milk, and sheep's milk.

FSAI has a great website: **www.fsai.ie**. It publishes for sale a *Safe Catering Pack*, with a DVD, which has all the documentation you need. You can also download the records forms free from the FSAI website.

The Food Standards Agency (FSA) is an independent non-ministerial Government Department. The EHOs are based in the Councils and so they are your first port of call if you are thinking about starting up a new food business – see **www.food.gov.uk/business-industry/hygieneratings/food-law-inspections.** You can register your new business online at **www.gov.uk/food-business-registration** and arrange for the Council to visit you to inspect and approve your kitchen and premises. The FSA website has a useful checklist for starting up, helping you think about many business issues (some of these issues are useful for any business, not just food): **www.food.gov.uk/business-industry/startingup.**

In Northern Ireland and the UK, you don't need to be inspected or approved if you sell directly to the public or to retailers like caterers, pubs and restaurants, as long as:

- Food is less than 25% of your trade;
- You don't handle any wild game meat products;
- You don't sell food outside the county your business is registered in.

However, you must be inspected and approved by your local Council if your business involves handling meat, fish, egg or dairy products.

The FSA website is really good too – the *Safe Catering Guide* mentioned above, a *Food Start-up Guide* and all the forms you need for recording your food safety are available free at **www.food.gov.uk.**

In Scotland, similar support is available from Food Standards Scotland (**www.foodstandards.gov.scot**).

Is Your Kitchen Good Enough?

Most modern kitchens are well-equipped to provide all that is needed to satisfy the requirements for kitchen production – in other words, you can start straight away. But you need to ensure that what you are making will not possibly pose a health risk to anyone who eats it. You are selling to the public now, so what might be OK for you and your family at home might not be OK for food being sold to paying consumers.

Simple things like keeping everything really clean and tidy, not having family or pets running around, being organised, keeping your food business ingredients separate from your household ingredients and so on will go a long way to getting your kitchen in order. Separation of home and work ingredients can be achieved very simply by having a dedicated cupboard or shelf, buying some big lunchboxes and sticking a label on them so that other members of the household don't use them or mess with them. If you don't have a space (or money) for a second fridge, and your EHO or Inspector says it's OK to do so, put your refrigerated food business ingredients into separate, labelled containers – "Hands Off Dad's / Mum's work ingredients" (and keep reminding yourself and your family that you're in business now!).

You'll need separate sinks for washing your hands and for washing utensils. Many modern kitchens have a little side sink between the main sink and the draining board. There you go – two sinks – or perhaps you have a second sink in a utility room.

You can't have any laundry in your kitchen – that means no washing machine – it should be in the utility room.

The other rumour that abounds is that you need everything tiled from floor to ceiling or else stainless steel everywhere. Not true! The legislation simply calls for all surfaces to be easily cleanable. In other words, smooth, non-porous, in good repair. If your kitchen counter is made from marble or Formica or similar, then that will be fine. If you have a wooden surface, then it shouldn't be deeply scored with knife marks as bacteria like the dirt that gets trapped in these, so the best thing is to use a plastic chopping board (although these can also get damaged by knives over time) or cover it with a plastic cloth if you're going to be working directly on it.

Best to remove all clutter from the area you're working in. If there are plants on the window sills, remove them while you're working in case they fall over and spill out onto your food or work surface.

If you are doing a lot of cooking that generates steam and condensation on your windows, you will need an extractor fan. Your hob or cooker hood might do the job. Your windows should be kept closed unless you're happy to put flyscreens on them.

Keep the dog, cat and children out while you're preparing food.

It's all pretty much common sense. The bottom line is that if you're not sure, ask your EHO or Inspector.

Finally, if your kitchen is approved but you find your oven is too small or your equipment is not suitable, then you might want to consider your options – see the next section. However, the solution might even be simpler than that – get up earlier in the morning. Seriously! One client of mine complained that her oven was too small and she couldn't supply to meet the demand. It turned out she only made one batch on a Sunday morning. Seems obvious I know, but sometimes even the obvious eludes us.

What If Your Kitchen Isn't Good Enough?

If you can't use your kitchen at home for some reason, whether through your own choice or if you've been inspected and you've been told that it's not suitable legally, or if the changes you have to make to get it up to standard are too much for you to do, or it's too small for the volume you're making, then what are your options?

One baker that I know started off using the kitchen in a pub that wasn't in use. The kitchen was perfectly serviceable and, after a good clean and the 'go ahead' from the EHO, he was in business, and the pub-owner was delighted to get some rental income. Another producer started off using a closed-down fast food place to make sandwiches for distribution to local schools and businesses. Someone else I know used the kitchen in a small café that was only open during the summer season – she started off there in the winter, just to get going, and then moved into bigger premises when she was up and running and had proved there was a market for her food (the proof being the fact that it was selling), and since the café was due to reopen for the summer, she was on a deadline.

A number of food units have been built around the country that can be rented by the hour, week or longer term. Local Enterprise Offices (LEOs), Councils, the LEADER companies (as everyone still calls them) and some community and private enterprises have built proper food units finished to food production standard that you can rent – contact your local Council, Community Office or Enterprise Office / Company to enquire. There are several across the UK (try Google to find them) and here is a selection on the island of Ireland:

- Castlehill Foods has a 900 sq. ft. (84m²) kitchen and food production premises available to hire outside Killala, Co. Mayo;

- Cork County Council operates Cork Incubator Kitchens (**www.corkincubatorkitchens.ie**);

- Enterprise Castlerea in Co. Roscommon is planning a new facility that will include a kitchen and units to rent, called *An Chistin*, in the Enterprise Hub (**www.castlereaenterprisehub.ie**).

- In Kilkenny, The School of Food offers a commercial kitchen for small or growing food businesses, professional chefs or home cooks to rent on a daily basis. Costs are €90 + VAT @ 23% per day or €45 + VAT @ 23% per half-day and include waste, electricity, sanitising solution for cleaning, gas and cleaning equipment (**www.schooloffood.ie/incubation-kitchen**);

- In Northern Ireland, the only Food Business Incubation Centre at the time of writing is situated at Loughry Campus in Cookstown, Co. Tyrone. The Centre was opened in 1998 and provides eight purpose-built food processing factory units finished to the highest standards in two sizes: 175m² and 225m² (**www.cafre.ac.uk**). There are plans to build a second food enterprise centre in Armagh;

- Meals on Wheels and other community kitchens that are not at full capacity may be available if you enquire locally;

- Moy Valley Resources IRD have clients occupying Enterprise Units at a number of locations around Ballina, Co. Mayo, for a mixture of both food and non-food producers (**www.moyvalley.ie**);

- Newmarket Kitchen has opened in Bray, Co. Wicklow and offers shared kitchen space on a membership basis (**www.newmarketkitchen.ie**);

- Nutgrove Enterprise Park, Dublin, has two high-spec food production units, each 59.45m² with own-door ground floor access and parking (**www.nutgrove-enterprisepark.ie / info@dlrceb.ie**);

- SPADE Enterprise Centre is a community-based enterprise centre in the converted St. Paul's Church at North King Street, Dublin (**www.spade.ie**);

- Terenure Enterprise Centre, Dublin, has three fully-serviced food units (**www.terenure-enterprise.ie**);

- The Ferbane Food Campus in Co. Offaly opened in 2003 (**www.ferbanefoodcampus.ie**);

- The Food Hub in Drumshanbo, Co. Leitrim is a shining example. Operational since 2004, the Food Hub provides 26,000 sq. ft. of premium food production space across 14 independent work units and its Community Kitchen is a timeshare production unit where start-up food businesses can make their foods in a fully-equipped kitchen, paying by the hour (currently €15/hour) with no commitment other than to bring your own ingredients (**www.thefoodhub.com**);

- The Limerick Food Centre at Raheen Business Park provides food manufacturing and processing units for commercial letting (**www.shannonproperties.ie**);

- The North Tipperary Food Works in Rearcross, Newport, Co. Tipperary was developed by North Tipperary Food Enterprise Centre (Rearcross) Ltd. An old creamery building was converted into a premium food workspace. There is a timeshare kitchen and production units for rental. At the time of writing, the cost of rental of the timeshare kitchen is €15 per hour + VAT for the fully equipped kitchen, which includes gas, water and electricity. The Food Production units cost €550 per month + VAT and, as a tenant, you kit them out yourself as well as taking over utility bills (**www.northtippfoodworks.ie**);

- Údarás na Gaeltachta has three food units in Co. Donegal (**www.udaras.ie**);

Bord Bia has published a list of units on **www.bordbiavantage.ie**.

Food Safety and Hygiene Legislation

Food safety and hygiene legislation is concerned about these four issues:

- The protection of health;
- Making sure that proper information is given (so that the consumer is properly informed);
- The prevention of fraud (horsemeat, anyone?);
- Freedom of trade (throughout the EU).

The last one isn't really a concern for you, day to day – nor, hopefully, the second last!

The legislation that applies generally to small food producers are *Regulations EC 178/2002* (which sets out the general requirements of food law and food safety), *EC 852/2004* (the Hygiene of Foodstuffs) and possibly *EC 853/2004* (specific hygiene rules for food of animal origin). There is also Irish legislation *S.I. 369 of 2006*, which is mostly about your responsibility as a food producer to comply with the law and about enforcement of the legislation.

If you read all the legislation, you'll possibly find yourself a little bewildered. It's a really good idea to ask someone to help you with this. If you're feeling brave, download a copy of *EC 852/2004* from **www.fsai.ie** and jump to *Annex II* to start. Go back and read the rest of it when you have drawn breath.

All food service providers, caterers, supermarkets and retailers require their food producers, processors and suppliers to comply with food safety legislation. In order to make sure that you address the concerns of your customers, and because it's the law, then you, as a new producer, must comply with the relevant quality and food safety regulations, and what's more, to be seen to be in compliance. This goes whether you decide to sell through shops or direct to the customer from your back door or through farmers' or country markets.

A good reference document is the *Guide to Food Law for Artisan / Small Food Producers Starting a New Business* available for free download from **www.fsai.ie**, which will direct you to all the legislation you need. Since it's all EU legislation, the guide can be used by food businesses in any EU country.

Jargon

You will find the definitions associated with food legislation in Article 2 of *EC 852/2004* and in Articles 2 and 3 of *EC 178/2002*. Here are a few:

- 'Food' (or 'foodstuff') means any substance or product, whether processed, partially processed or unprocessed, intended to be ... ingested by humans. 'Food' includes drink, chewing gum and any substance, including water, that is intentionally incorporated into the food during its manufacture, preparation or treatment. It includes bottled drinking water. (*Regulation 178/2002* also tells you what is not food!);

- 'Food law' means the laws and regulations governing food in general, and food safety in particular. It covers any stage of production, processing and distribution of food, and also of feed produced for, or fed to, food-producing animals;

- A 'food business' means any undertaking, whether for profit or not and whether public or private, carrying out any of the activities related to any stage of production, processing and distribution of food;

- A 'food business operator' means the person(s) responsible for ensuring that the requirements of food law are met within the food business under their control – that's you if you are a food producer!

- 'Food hygiene', or 'hygiene', means the measures and conditions necessary to control hazards and to ensure fitness for human consumption of a foodstuff, taking into account its intended use;

- 'Primary products' means products of primary production, including products of the soil (growing fruit or vegetables, in other words), of stock farming, of hunting and fishing;

- 'Establishment' means any unit of a food business;
- 'Competent authority' means the FSAI, HSE, DAFM, FSA, FSS, etc.;
- 'Contamination' means the presence or introduction of a hazard;
- A 'hazard' can be either physical, chemical or microbiological;
- 'Wrapping' means the placing of a foodstuff in a wrapper or container in *direct contact* with the foodstuff concerned, and the wrapper or container itself;
- 'Packaging' means the placing of one or more wrapped foodstuffs in a second outer container, and that outer container itself;
- 'Processing' means any action that substantially alters the initial product, including heating, smoking, curing, maturing, drying, marinating, extraction, extrusion or a combination of those processes;
- 'Unprocessed products' means foodstuffs that have not undergone processing, and includes products that have been divided, parted, severed, sliced, boned, minced, skinned, ground, cut, cleaned, trimmed, husked, milled, chilled, frozen, deep-frozen or thawed;
- 'Processed products' means foodstuffs resulting from the processing of unprocessed products. These products may contain ingredients that are necessary for their manufacture or to give them specific characteristics;
- 'HACCP' means Hazard Analysis and Critical Control Point (see later in this chapter);
- 'Unsafe food' – Article 14 of *Regulation EC 178/2002* requires that food must not be placed on the market if it is unsafe. Food shall be deemed to be unsafe if it is considered to be injurious to health or unfit for human consumption;
- 'Traceability' – food business operators must be able to identify any person from whom they have been supplied with a food, a food-producing animal, or food ingredient. You must have a system and procedures in place to manage your traceability. It's straightforward, but critical (see below for more detail);

- 'The hygiene package' is the bundle of food legislation applied since 1 January 2006, when existing legislation was revised and rationalised to introduce consistency and clarity throughout the food production chain from 'farm to fork'.

Registration

The law says that, before commencing trading, a food business operator (FBO) – that's you – must register with a competent authority – that's either with the Environmental Health office in your local HSE (Republic of Ireland) or Council (UK and NI) office. Failure to do so is an offence! Businesses that handle and / or process foods of animal origin need approval from the appropriate competent authority, either the DAFM or Council. Once you get in contact, they will go through the details of the approval process with you. In the UK and NI, this can be done online.

If you're not sure which one applies to you, just phone one of them and if it's not them, they'll direct you to the right body! As I've said above, unless you're farm-based or are making cheese for example, it will usually be the EHOs that you need to talk to.

It is really a good idea to contact them for advice sooner rather than later. Approval of your kitchen will take into account the kitchen layout, whether it is easy to clean, where you keep your rubbish (waste management), how you make your foods (processes), food safety (HACCP), your product range and how much you are making (volumes), for a start.

The reason the inspector considers the volume of food you make is that, while you might be able to manage small amounts now, things might get out of control and be hard or impossible to manage if you get too busy. If this busy-ness causes a risk for food safety, then you'll have to make some changes. However, cross that bridge when you come to it. (By the way, being busy because of demand is a good thing for you – it means you are selling lots!).

Traceability

Traceability is quite simply knowing who you bought what from and who you sold it on to if you're selling it to another business, such as a restaurant or retailer. However, when you're selling directly to the consumer, through a farmers' market or your own shop or in a restaurant, then you don't need to know the names and addresses of all your customers!

You must keep a list of the suppliers you use regularly. The best way to do this is have a sheet that you fill every time you buy ingredients or packaging – see **www.fsai.ie** or **www.bordbiavantage.ie** or **www.food.gov.uk** for examples or just create one yourself.

As a food producer, you should ensure that you use reliable and reputable suppliers and that the products you buy meet your own standards. One way to achieve this is for you to have an agreed product specification with your supplier, including the temperature at which the product must be transported and delivered, the condition of packaging, the correct labelling, and so on.

If you buy poor quality ingredients or raw materials that cause a problem for you in the long run, then it is to you that the customer will complain. It is your reputation that's on the line. The customer is not interested in the fact that one of your suppliers is at fault; all they see is your name on the food that caused illness or problems. So, don't let poor standards from your suppliers result in poor standards for your foods. Also, make sure your suppliers are registered themselves with the HSE or whoever, and ask for a copy of their approval certificate for your own files.

In summary:

- All businesses must be able to identify their suppliers (supplier traceability) – what you bought, when you bought it, its batch code and expiry date;
- Businesses supplying their product *to other businesses* must be able to identify their customers (customer traceability);
- Any food that is placed on the market must be adequately labelled to ensure traceability throughout the food chain – what you sold,

when you sold it, its batch code and its expiry date (your shelf life date can sometimes double up as your batch code).

What Is HACCP?

When you are selling food to the general public, you must make sure that your food is safe. In other words, that it won't cause any food poisoning, that it is fit for human consumption and that it is not injurious to health. In order to show that you are in control of what you're doing, then the law (*Regulation EC 852/2004*) says that you must put in some sort of system or procedures to prove it (and if you are dealing with foods of animal origin, then you must also comply with *Regulation EC 853/2004*, don't forget).

HACCP stands for 'Hazard Analysis and Critical Control Point' and is the most common and best-recognised procedure for food safety and hygiene. In the simplest terms, it means that you identify where something might go wrong (that could result in unsafe food) and specify what you would do about it to prevent it from happening. You want to make sure the food is not contaminated by any bacteria or bits of hair or pieces of anything that shouldn't be in there. If it's not in the recipe, it shouldn't be in the food!

If you go to the trouble of putting procedures in place, then for goodness sake record it and get the credit for it! And if you do record it, make sure it has been done – don't go filling in forms if the job hasn't been done first.

Depending on the food you are producing, the EHO or Inspector may or may not insist that you do formal HACCP training. Look out for courses in your area – see **Chapter 9** for more information.

HACCP prerequisites

Before implementing HACCP, basic food hygiene conditions and practices referred to as 'prerequisites' must be in place. HACCP then can be used by the business to identify steps that are critical in ensuring the preparation of safe food and which need tight control and monitoring. Prerequisites include:

- Cleaning and sanitation (regular cleaning of premises and equipment);
- Maintenance (repairs and routine maintenance of premises and equipment);
- Personal hygiene (hand-washing);
- Pest control (vents and any external windows that open in the food preparation areas fitted with a flyscreen / repair any gaps and cracks);
- Equipment (use equipment that can be thoroughly cleaned and taken apart if necessary);
- Premises and structure (the size of the premises – your kitchen or garage conversion – must be enough to handle the volume of food you are making);
- Services (a potable water supply – if your water comes from a well or private supply such as a group scheme, then you'll need to get it tested);
- Storage, distribution and transport (storage of foods at the correct temperature / make sure raw and ready-to-eat foods are separated);
- Waste management (removing waste frequently to prevent it becoming a source of food contamination) – don't let it pile up;
- Zoning (physical separation of activities to prevent potential food contamination) – this applies if you are making cooked or other high-risk foods, or if you are washing vegetables.

Has All This Started to Put You Off Yet?

Don't worry, it's really not that difficult to manage all of this when you are operating on a small scale. It looks like a long list but a lot of it is common-sense – you are just making sure that there is no dirt that bugs can grow in and that your food won't get contaminated with bacteria or something falling into it. Just make sure everything is clean and tidy, in good order, that you and anyone working with you are also clean and hygienic.

Once you have got the prerequisites sorted, then it is time to get on with looking at the 'seven principles of HACCP'. These are the steps that you take when organising your HACCP plan – get help with this from a training course or food safety advisor or your EHO / Inspector, or from the FSAI or FSA start-up pack.

The steps are:

- **Identify the hazards:** If you're lucky, there might not be any hazards!
- **Determine the critical control points (CCPs):** If there is a hazard, what can you do to prevent it becoming a problem for you?
- **Establish critical limit(s):** What's your limit? It might be an upper or lower temperature, for example. Or if you are making high-risk foods that need microbiological testing, then it will be the lab that will let you know what the result is and whether it's a problem;
- **Establish a system to monitor control of the CCPs:** How do you check? Perhaps use a thermometer or a temperature probe for your fridge or for checking the inside of cooked food, for example;
- **Establish the corrective action to be taken when monitoring indicates that a particular CCP is not under control:** If something goes wrong, what do you do? You might just throw it out and start again, you might turn down your fridge temperature setting, or turn up the heat on the cooker, or leave it to cook for longer so that it reaches the right temperature throughout, depending on what it is you are checking up on;
- **Establish procedures for verification to confirm the HACCP system is working effectively:** Do some random spot checks now and then;
- **Establish documentation concerning all procedures and records appropriate to these principles and their application:** Write it all down in your HACCP record forms.

HACCP Records

For HACCP to work successfully and to satisfy the inspectors, records must be kept and be readily available as evidence. The number of records you need will depend very much on the types of foods you are making and complexity of your business. The aim should be to ensure control is maintained without generating excessive paperwork. Ask your EHO or Inspector for guidance.

Again, the *Safe Catering Pack* is very handy for learning about HACCP and gives you all the forms you need to keep your records. FSAI also has a booklet, *HACCP Terminology Explained*, that you can download for free from the FSAI website. The FSA has a very good free guide called '*Food Hygiene – A Guide for Businesses*' on its website and a great online tool called *MyHACCP*. Don't panic, it's not rocket science!

Low Risk and High Risk

A low-risk food is one that is unlikely to be a risk to public health – in other words, cause food poisoning – usually because they are acidic (like pickle) or don't contain much water (like bread or jam) so bacteria can't grow easily. Low-risk foods spoil due to their chemical composition (not microbiological activity) and usually have a 'Best Before' date. Bread, cake, buns, jam are all low-risk generally.

High-risk foods on the other hand are much more at risk of microbial contamination, particularly harmful bacteria called pathogens. These foods are generally refrigerated or frozen, and have a 'Use By' date. Examples include seafood, freshly prepared salads, or ready-to-eat (RTE) foods such as quiche, cooked foods, some meats and dairy products. The main reason these are high-risk is because they may be eaten without any further cooking or processing, so if they are contaminated with food poisoning bacteria, then the consumer is at risk. However, even if the food is going to be cooked by the consumer before it is eaten, that is also considered high-risk.

If you have a sponge cake that you sandwich together with a fresh cream filling, it increases the risk. The sponge itself is low-risk, but because the cream is a dairy product and can go off (spoilage bacteria will grow) unless it's refrigerated, then that increases the risk. When to use Best Before and Use By dates is covered in **Chapter 7**.

Conclusion

It's understandable that a new producer just starting up may find the legislation all a bit overwhelming. Don't feel you need to know the legislation inside out and have it all at your fingertips. Just know what you need for your foods.

But that's the problem! How do I know what I need for my food? Ask your EHO or Inspector for advice. You can also ask your Local Enterprise Office (**www.localenterprise.ie**) or Enterprise Unit in your Council to give you a food business mentor (this is often a free service) – just make sure your mentor knows the legislation. You'll get to know it all yourself well enough in good time.

4

ENSURING FOOD SAFETY AND HYGIENE

Basic Microbiology

A micro-organism (microbe) is a creature that is invisible to the human eye and can be seen only under a microscope. A dot on a page the size of a full stop would contain millions of them. Microbes are found everywhere – in your hair, throat, nose, gut and hands; in the soil and air; on surfaces; in food, shellfish, water, vegetables, plants … and the word used to describe this is 'ubiquitous'.

There are five types: bacteria, viruses, moulds, yeasts and fungi. Some of these microbes are useful and good for us – for example:

- Bacteria (*Lactobacilli*) aid digestion;
- Fungi (mushrooms) are edible;
- Moulds produce antibiotics (penicillin), and are used in making cheese (Brie rind);
- Viruses are used to make vaccines and in research;
- Yeasts are used in brewing beer, baking bread and other fermented foods.

Most bacteria are harmless but many are responsible for disease, illness and infection. Harmful bacteria are known as pathogens:

- Bacteria (sometimes called 'germs' or 'bugs') can cause food poisoning and thus illness;
- Fungi cause food spoilage;
- Moulds also cause food spoilage (for example, on bread or cheese);
- Viruses can cause food poisoning;

- Yeasts – too many can contaminate liquids.

Many bacteria are capable of forming spores – a protective shell that helps them to survive when food is scarce. You are probably familiar with tetanus or 'lock jaw'. Tetanus is an infection of the nervous system by the potentially deadly bacteria *Clostridium tetani*. Spores of the bacteria live in the soil. In the spore form, C. *tetani* may remain inactive in the soil, as if it is hibernating, but it can remain infectious for more than 40 years. So that's why if you get soil in a cut, you need to wash it out straight away, or get a tetanus shot, just in case.

What Do Bacteria Need to Grow?

Bacteria need six things to grow:

- **Time:** Bacteria divide in half (and so double in number) every 20 minutes under the right conditions;
- **Warmth:** The best temperature for them to grow is 37°C (body temperature) but they can grow in temperatures anywhere from 5°C to 63°C, known as the 'danger zone';
- **Oxygen:** For some bacteria (aerobic), but others grow without it (anaerobic bacteria);
- **Food:** Protein, which could be proper food or just dirt;
- **Moisture:** Water;
- **pH (acid / alkali conditions):** Bacteria dislike extremes so they won't grow where it's too acidic (on pickles) or too alkaline (which is why soap works to clean them away).

How Do I Control the Growth of Bacteria?

Simply put, if you can control some or all of the six things above – time, warmth, oxygen, food, moisture and pH – then you will do well.

As a rule of thumb, keep hot food hot, keep cold food cold (refrigerated at 5°C or below). Food must be cooked to 75°C or hotter. Do not leave hot food sitting around for too long where it will start to cool; if the temperature of the food is at less than 63°C for more than two hours, then you have to throw it out. Put food in the fridge as soon as possible. You might preserve some foods by removing oxygen (for example, by bottling it, or putting it in jars, or canning it). Lack of moisture in some foods will prevent bacteria growing in them (jam, preserves, dried foods). Vegetables can be preserved by controlling the pH, which is how pickling developed (the acid in the vinegar isn't suitable for most bacteria to grow). Finally, preserving foods by smoking (for example, smoked salmon) is one of the world's oldest methods of slowing microbial growth. However, smoking alone isn't usually sufficient to get any decent shelf life and is usually helped by vacuum packing.

Don't feed the bugs (clean to remove dirt) and don't leave damp cleaning cloths or mops about where bugs can start to grow.

What are Some Common Types of Bacteria?

You might have heard of Salmonella, E. coli, *Clostridium perfringens* (one of the main causes of food poisoning), *Clostridium difficile* (sometimes referred to as *C. diff.*) which is a hospital-acquired infection, *Clostridium botulinum* (causes botulism – also used in Botox, by the way, as it acts by paralysing the muscle), *Campylobacter, Staphylococcus* or *Streptococcus*.

Most *E. coli* strains are harmless, but some can cause serious food poisoning. The harmless strains are part of the normal flora of the gut. The bad news is that, even if the harmless ones are found in food, it shows that the food has been contaminated with faeces. Yuck!

Most *Staphylococci* are harmless and are normally found on the skin and mucous membranes of humans (inside the nose) and other animals. So, if it's in your food, it possibly means that someone hasn't been washing their hands after blowing their nose. Eeeooow!

While many types of *Streptococcus* are harmless, you will be familiar with the one that causes 'Strep throat'. If *Streptococcus* is found in your food, it possibly means that someone may have coughed into your food or hasn't been washing their hands after coughing. Not nice!

What is Food Poisoning?

Food poisoning is an illness that occurs usually between six and 36 hours after eating poisonous or contaminated food. Symptoms include vomiting, nausea, diarrhoea, abdominal pain and even death in extreme cases.

Food poisoning can be caused by bacteria, viruses, chemicals, metals (such as lead or mercury) and poisonous plants, such as the foxglove (*digitalis*) or poisonous mushrooms or toadstools.

Case Study – Jonathan and Maria's Wedding

I attended the wedding of friends a few years ago in England. The reception was held in their local village hall and the food – a buffet of cold meats and salads – was catered by family and friends. The next day, all 58 guests, and the newly-married couple, suffered a really bad dose of food poisoning. Four people were hospitalised, as they were severely ill. Due to the large number of people affected, the incident was notified to Staffordshire Council and an investigation ensued. The offending food was not identified, which meant no fingerpointing at the unfortunate person who had prepared it, but it was most likely a pasta salad, where the pasta was not completely cold before being mixed with mayonnaise or tuna or meat. It just shows that food poisoning can happen easily and can just as easily affect a large number of people. Bad enough that this would happen at a wedding, but just imagine if this was your food business!

How Do I Reduce Bacteria in the Food I Make?

There are three ways to reduce bacteria in the food you make:

- **Food hygiene management:** To make sure the food does not get contaminated;
- **Personal hygiene management:** Keeping yourself and your staff / helpers clean;
- **Environmental hygiene management:** Keeping your equipment, and workplace clean and tidy.

Each of these will be controlled by your HACCP system that we discussed earlier. When you do your food hygiene training (which is required by law), then all will be explained in more detail.

Hygiene

Hygiene refers to the practices and procedures essential to the maintenance of health and the quality of life – keeping things clean and uncontaminated, in other words.

Why Bother?

If you don't have good hygiene practices when you prepare food, then you run the risk of causing food poisoning. That's not good for your customer and not good for your reputation or your business.

Personal Hygiene

Good personal hygiene includes keeping your body clean (shower regularly), washing your hands regularly, wearing clean clothes and not engaging in unhygienic practices such as smoking, coughing or sneezing over food or people, picking your nose, ears, cuts, etc., nail-biting, using your finger to taste food, double-dipping (using a spoon to taste, licking it, then dipping the same spoon into the food again without washing it first) or spitting.

The big thing to remember here is WASH YOUR HANDS! You must always wash your hands:

- **Before:**
  - o Starting work;
  - o Handling food;
  - o You move on to the next task;
- **Before and after:**
  - o Treating wounds or cuts;
  - o Touching a sick or injured person;
  - o Inserting or removing contact lenses;
- **After:**
  - o Using the toilet;

- o Handling raw food, especially meat;
- o Touching your face, nose, ears, hair, mouth, cuts;
- o Smoking;
- o Handling waste;
- o Cleaning duties;
- o Meal breaks;
- o Sneezing, coughing, or blowing your nose;
- o Handling money (just think about where money has been!)

A carrier is a person who harbours, and may pass on, harmful bacteria, even though that person may show no signs of illness. If this person has poor personal hygiene and they handle food, then they might easily pass on the harmful bacteria to someone else.

5

PRODUCT DEVELOPMENT

Introduction

Wherever you get your ideas or whatever your motivation, you need to think things through before ploughing ahead. The more time, thought and energy that you give to this at the start, then the higher your chances of success.

Your resources (financial, human, facilities) are limited, especially at the beginning of a project. So, it is important to spend resources wisely: by being careful from the start, you will ensure that there will be enough time, cash and energy to keep going.

Questions you should consider:

- **What are you going to make / produce / sell?** This is your first priority. Be clear what you want to do and why you want to do it. It will work out best if you enjoy what you are doing, and are good at it. Ideally, when looking at the local market, see whether there is a gap that you can fill with your delicious food. For example, despite a competitive market, there are still market opportunities for Irish ice cream-makers. Ice cream is often regarded as an 'affordable indulgence' and suits the trend towards home entertainment;

- **Who / what is your target market?** Is it families, individuals, older people, children, single people, married couples, men, women, healthy eaters, dieters, indulgers, students, workers …? Don't make the mistake of thinking that everyone is your target market. Different groups like different things.

- **Who are your competitors?** Everyone has a competitor. Even
  makers of sausages with high meat content have competition from
  poorer quality sausages – if the consumer is offered a choice, they
  may go for the cheaper option, despite it being lower quality,
  depending on their budget. Know who your competitors are,
  where they are, and how you might steal away some of their
  customers! Carry out a benchmarking exercise: What do your
  competitors do well that you might do too, and what are their
  weaknesses? You can compete with them by shouting about your
  strengths, the great traits / flavours / quality of your food.

- **How will you make the cheese / bread / jam / hummus?** Can you
  get the necessary ingredients? Do you want to use organic
  ingredients? Will your customers pay extra for them? Will
  changing an ingredient impact positively or negatively on your
  food – will it taste better or worse? Have you a recipe and method?
  Does it work for bigger batches?

- **What equipment / premises are needed?** Do you need any
  specialised equipment? Will your existing kitchen equipment do or
  must you buy new equipment? Do you need a new fridge? Have
  you enough cupboard space? Is everything cleanable? **(Chapter 3)**;

- **Where will your food be sold?** You could start by providing a
  local service to build recognition – collections from your house,
  deliver to local shops or supermarkets, sell at farmers' / country
  markets and agricultural shows and music / cultural events. Sell
  online. Where do your competitors sell their goods? Will you be
  there too? (see **Chapter 6**);

- **How much should you charge?** You need to compare the selling
  price of your food to similar products on the market. The
  consumer may expect to pay more for artisan food, but you need to
  prove it's worth the extra. Also, make sure you are not
  undercharging – don't forget to work out how much it costs you to
  make it (ingredients, electricity, packaging, your time, distribution)
  so that you don't make a loss (see **Chapter 8**);

- **Where and when will the food be eaten?** Meal times, picnics, on-
  the-go, special occasions ... this will affect the way you present and

package the food, whether you put one, two or six items in a pack for example, as well as the type of packaging itself. If the travelling public is your market, eating on-the-go or 'dashboard dining', then remember to think about what portion size and packaging will best suit someone having lunch at their desk or in their car;

- **What are your packaging options?** Can you use plastic, paper, recyclable / green credentials, glass, jars, tubs or bags? How many items should you put in a pack? Should you offer the option of single packs and multi-packs? If your food is already in shops, then think about pack sizes, formats and packaging for existing lines;

- **Is the product seasonal?** How do you manage in winter or off-season? Can you buy-in ingredients from elsewhere when you don't have them in your own garden, for example? Can you adapt the product for different times of year? Can you introduce limited edition or seasonal varieties such as a turkey and ham pie at Christmas, lamb and mint for Easter, or bacon and cabbage for St. Patrick's Day?

- **How much of an income can you hope to get from making and selling these foods?** Is this going to be extra money for you or do you want to have a business that will provide you with a proper income? Either way, you must work out your costs (this is all covered in detail in **Chapter 8**).

New Product Development

Once you decide what it is you want to make, then spend some time developing your recipe and method. Do plenty of trials to make sure you can manage making just more than one or two at a time. Your kitchen equipment might be fine at the beginning, but might not last if you are using it long term or for larger sizes / quantities. Or your recipe may not scale – for example, if you increase the size of a cake from 6" to 9" or 12", and you use the same recipe, it might not turn out the same. You may have to alter your recipe and method for larger sizes – trial and error again.

You might have heard about new product development (NPD) models or perhaps the phrase 'stage gate'. These are just ways of managing the way in which new foods, or indeed any new products, are developed. The idea behind any development system is to make sure you avoid wasting your resources (time, energy, money, mental health!) as far as you can.

Typical steps are:

- **Idea generation stage:** How to come up with new ideas (see above);
- **Feasibility stage:** Desk research, check out the market – is there anyone else local doing what you want to do? Look at your resources: do you have the time, money, knowledge, ability, kitchen, equipment etc. that you need? Perhaps you should do a full-scale feasibility study before going too much further. Consider the following:
  - Technical – *can I make it?*
    - Product development
    - Operations
  - Commercial – *can I sell it?*
    - Target market
    - Routes to market
    - Distribution
  - Financial – *can I make a profit?*
    - Costs
    - Sales projections
    - Cash flows
    - Profit & loss
  - Team – *who is going to do it?*
    - Third parties
    - Roles and responsibilities
    - Risk analysis;
- **Concept development:** Produce samples, do trials, test them out on your family and friends. Move on to bigger batches, check any technical issues (you may need to tweak your recipe, like in the cake example above);

- **Business case:** This stage includes a more detailed look at your target market, sales (how and where are you going to sell your food?), production (how and where are you going to make it?), human resources (will it be just you or will you have help, and who is going to do what?) and financial issues (can you afford to start-up? Can you get a grant? What are your financial projections and what about cash flow?) (see **Chapter 8** for more about money);
- **Launch:** Introduce your new product to the market – in effect, this probably means putting a few loaves, jars, buns, cakes or whatever into your car or the basket of your bicycle and bringing them up to the corner shop where your local friendly shopkeeper has agreed to take a few to try them out and see whether they sell;
- **Review:** Look back over everything now and then and see whether you want to make any changes. Can you get cheaper / better ingredients? Can you make bigger batches? Can you add to the range? Can you save on costs anywhere without compromising your quality?

Processing Partners – Outsourcing Production

Consider a simple question: Will you make your food product yourself or get someone else to do it for you?

It is not unreasonable to consider outsourcing some of your production work. You might buy in readymade pastry cases, for example – unless you are very keen to make your own, and if you make really good pastry, then go ahead. However, it is possible to buy very good quality frozen pastry, so don't rule it out. Some of the top chefs in the country buy-in their pastry.

If you are making sausages or meat products, you might develop the recipe and specify the ingredients, but perhaps you don't have a sausage machine. You could ask a butcher to make the sausages for you or ask if you can have access to the machine when it's not in use.

The golden rule of any 'partnership' is trust and making sure that you can work with people for the long-term. The trust derived from business relationships offers far more security than anything written down in a contract. All the same, you should ask your sub-contractor (the person / company who is going to make the food for you) to sign a non-disclosure agreement, which would give you some protection, but you should be aware that even a slight tweak to a recipe or a process might render this agreement null and void.

One step you should definitely take is to document your recipe and the detail of the required processes and send both to yourself by registered post and DO NOT OPEN the envelope unless you find yourself in a litigation process and only then open the package in a legal setting – solicitor's office or courtroom – with independent witnesses present. This is the most cost-effective method of proving ownership of the intellectual property (IP) for small businesses.

Sensory Analysis

How does the food taste, look, smell and feel? Dark chocolate snaps when you break it because it has a high percentage of cocoa solids. Or does anyone remember Space Rocks, which popped and fizzed in your mouth? These are called the 'organoleptic' properties of food and assessing them is what we call 'sensory analysis'.

If you ever watch cookery programmes on television, you might notice that the good chefs taste their food as they go along. They want to make sure that there is a good balance of flavours, that it is seasoned correctly, that no one ingredient is overpowering – and they make adjustments accordingly. The same goes for the foods you are making for your new business. As you develop your recipe, taste it! Ask others to taste it too. Ideally, your tasters would be able to describe what they are tasting rather than simply saying they like it or don't like it without articulating why. Smokers do not make good tasters, by the way, as their taste buds are not sensitive enough.

Sensory analysis of food uses the five senses – sight, smell, taste, touch and hearing – either individually or in combination, to look at the characteristics of food:

- Appearance (sight);
- Flavour (taste and touch);
- Aroma (smell);

- Texture or 'mouthfeel' (touch)
- Sound (hearing).

Appearance

We eat with our eyes first, so is your food visually appealing? Think about the colour, size, shape and shine. The colour of food is very important: does it look natural or artificial? Bright green vegetables look fresher, for example. The shape, size and appearance also influence consumers. When is mould acceptable? Fine in a blue cheese but not on bread! Wilted lettuce or carrots that have a wizened appearance are not acceptable either. Good chocolate should be shiny, not dull.

Flavour

The flavour is sensed by the taste buds on the tongue and is actually a combination of taste and touch / texture. There are four types of taste sensation: sweet; salt; sour; and bitter.

By the way, sour and bitter tastes are often confused, so you need to be clear what your tasters mean when they describe the taste to you. Lemon juice has a sour taste, whereas coffee has a bitter taste.

Aroma

Smell detects the aroma of food – the smell of freshly baked bread, coffee, onions or bacon frying, for example – and is important in the appreciation of flavour. A pleasant aroma makes food appetising. Smell is also useful in detecting fresh, rancid or occasionally poisonous food.

Texture / Mouthfeel

Texture – how the food feels in your mouth – is a key quality for many foods – for example, think of the tenderness of meat, the softness of bread, the crunch when breaking into crème brulée or the chewiness of toffee. It includes the consistency, viscosity (thick or thin liquids), brittleness, chewiness and the size and shape of particles in food, like lumpy mashed potato or the texture of a pear that is gritty. The coldness of ice cream or the burning sensation of chilli are also considered to be textures, and they contribute to the overall flavour.

Sound

The sounds made by food during preparation and while eating it are important for consumers' decisions also, like the sizzle of fried food, the fizz of drinks, the crunch of raw vegetables, the cracking of hard biscuits or dark chocolate.

So, it is really very important to taste your food, to get others to taste it and to give you feedback and then to adjust your recipes as necessary.

Shelf Life

When you have developed your recipe, and are happy with the end result, you will have to work out the Best Before or Use By date for the label. One of the best explanations I've heard to describe the difference between 'Best Before' and 'Use By' dates is that used by SafeFood: *Best Before is a guideline and Use By is a deadline* (**www.safefood.eu**)

Shelf life tells the consumer how long food can be kept before it starts to deteriorate. However, the consumer must follow the stated storage conditions if the shelf life is to be achieved.

Is Shelf Life Related to Food Quality?

Yes, the food might be safe to eat after the expiry (Best Before) date, but it might be stale or mushy or flavourless. Since the Best Before date is related to quality (for example, taste, aroma, appearance), after that date the food may not be unsafe to eat, but it may not be pleasant to eat. Best Before is applied to foods that are low risk or are canned, frozen or dried, for example – usually foods that have a long shelf life.

Is Shelf Life Related to Food Safety?

Yes, absolutely! You use HACCP (**Chapter 3**) to help control the growth of pathogens (bad bacteria). The Use By date is all about the safety of a food product. In other words, is it safe to eat? It is very important for perishable foods that may pose a danger to human health after a short time. The accuracy of the Use By date is really important from a food safety point of view. Foods with a Use By date generally have a short shelf life.

How to Work Out the Shelf Life of Your Food

Shelf life testing works out how long a food will retain its quality during storage. The extent to which you have to do a 'shelf life study' depends on the food you are producing. Factors influencing shelf life of food include microbial growth (mould, bacteria, yeasts, etc.) and non-microbial spoilage caused due to the gain or loss of moisture from the food; any chemical changes that might occur; light-induced change (colour fading); temperature changes (which cause the whitening or 'bloom' in chocolate); physical damage that might occur over time if it gets crumbly or cracks form; or even other spoilage from rodents and insects, taint or tampering.

All these factors should be taken into account when working out your shelf life. If you are making low-risk foods like bread, jam, dips, etc., where public health is not a major issue, your own experience will inform you as to what the shelf life might be. For high-risk foods, though, you will have to send samples away to a microbiology lab for testing to measure how many bacteria are present that you need to worry about. Check with your inspector if you're unsure as to whether you need to test your foods.

Can you carry out your own shelf life testing? Yes, you can do it easily for some types of foods, especially those where it's the eating quality that you are concerned about. Simply store the food in its packaging under the storage conditions it should be kept in, then take a sample every day or week or as often as you need to notice any changes. This will give you a guide as to when the food starts to deteriorate, and you can set the shelf life accordingly. If you're not sure, or if your food is perishable and where food safety is the issue, then get professional advice.

By law, you must state the Best Before or Use By date on your label. This is covered in detail in **Chapter 7.**

6

ROUTES TO MARKET, BRANDING AND MARKETING

What is a Route to Market?

The 'route to market' is how you get your food onto consumers' tables, whether directly or through shops. The first step in finding the best routes to market for you is to think about the food itself, and what might suit it. For example, could you post it or is it too delicate / heavy? Will it have to be refrigerated or frozen? Also think about who you want to sell it to: they are your target customer. Now ask yourself: Where are they located? How are you going to get your food into their shopping bag – and onto their tables?

You should write down a short statement or business pitch that you will use to all your potential customers and retailers. It's good to prepare this in advance and be very familiar with it yourself since it will help you to be consistent rather than stumbling over your words every time you try to talk to someone about your new food venture. Include a clear description of the food's unique selling points (USPs). Practice saying it out loud, hear how it sounds.

The location and nature of your target market will influence which route to market you use. For most small-scale producers, the market is their local or regional area to begin with, selling to consumers who prefer local food and who are willing to pay a premium for it.

Where Are Your Customers?

Before you even start thinking about your best route to market, ask yourself: Where do my potential customers shop? If you only sell in farmers' and country markets, are you missing out on a large number of shoppers who only shop in supermarkets? Where are people going anyway that you might be able to sell from? Consider regional airports, where travellers are always keen to take something back home either for themselves or to bring as a gift; tourist attractions where there are large numbers of people herding through the gift shops and cafés; museums … could you sell there? Well, you won't know unless you ask!

The development of garage forecourt shops in recent years has been extraordinary. Gone, for the most part, are the little draughty huts with a shivering petrol pump attendant. Instead, there are elaborate shops selling everything from windscreen wash to wine – these present an opportunity too.

The Supply Chain

It is important for food businesses to understand the supply chain with which they are involved. There are usually two types:

- Retailers (for consumer foods);
- Food service (business to business or catering).

Alternative supply chains involve direct sales to consumers and many small producers start with this route – because it is short and simple. Direct sales can include farmers' markets and online selling.

The diagram below shows two typical supply chains. There are three steps in the process between farm and consumer: each step in the process takes a slice of the 'money pie'. By using the direct sales route, some of the steps are eliminated, and with them, some of the costs.

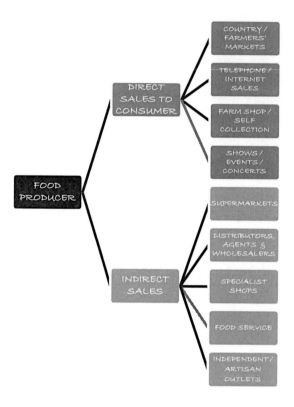

Route Options

There are two main routes to market categories:

- **Direct sales** – from you *direct to the consumer (direct customer)*:
  - Country / farmers' markets;
  - Telephone / online sales – website, box schemes;
  - Farm shop / self-collection by consumer;
  - Shows / events / concerts
- **Indirect sales** – from you *to your business customer*
  - Supermarkets;
  - Distributors, agents and wholesalers;
  - Specialist shops (butchers, bakers, fruit and vegetables);
  - Food service (hotels, cafes, restaurants, pubs);
  - Food service (catering);
  - Independent retailers / specialist shops / artisan outlets.

Direct Sales

Farmers' (outdoor) and Country (indoor) markets provide direct access to customers. This route is good for getting customer feedback and for carrying out initial tests of market / product and a great many small producers use this route to market successfully. Farmers' markets attract local trade, bringing consumers who are concerned about mass-produced food, about supporting local producers, and who are keen to minimise food miles. These consumers are willing to pay extra for these benefits. These are the 'foodies'.

At the last count, there were approximately 175 farmers' and country markets operating across the Republic of Ireland (up from 130 four years ago), according to Bord Bia, with a further additional 10 at least in Northern Ireland (**www.discovernorthernireland.com**), and 52 farmers' markets in Scotland. In London alone, there are 20 (**www.lfm.org.uk**)! The successful markets are those that get plenty of customers (good footfall), attract regular customers who buy every week, have producers that offer good quality foods for sale consistently and are well managed.

If you decide to try this route, then you need to be aware of the rules and regulations that markets apply to producers. In Ireland, there is a *Voluntary Code of Good Practice for Farmers' Markets* available from Bord Bia (**www.bordbia.ie**). There is also lots of useful information in *The Village Market Handbook* from Irish Village Markets, which you can download free from the FSAI website (**www.fsai.ie**) or from **www.irishvillagemarkets.ie**. Bord Bia also publishes *A Guide to Selling Through Farmers' Markets, Farm Shops and Box Schemes in Ireland*, which again you can find on the Bord Bia website. Scottish Farmers' Markets, in conjunction with the FSA, has published *Selling at a Scottish Farmers' Market – The First Steps*, and the London website has something similar.

It is important to realise that, for most markets:

- Traders must carry their own public liability insurance – see **Chapter 8** for information about insurance;
- Not all markets provide canopies and tables, so you might have to bring your own every time;

- Traders involved in the handling of food must comply with food safety legislation of course, and some markets may ask you to show your HACCP approval certificate. There are some published guidelines for food stalls, so ask your Inspector or EHO.

Standing at a food stall is labour-intensive – it requires commitment in terms of stall staffing and management – and cash handing may be a risk factor.

From the perspective of the small food producer, direct selling *via* farmers' markets, box schemes and farm shops offers a number of advantages as a route to market. The supply chain is relatively short and there is direct contact with customers. This is a good way to start to build relationships with your customers, who will then recognise your food when they see it in their local shops. It also allows you to display your food the way you want it displayed, as you're not relying on shops to do a good job for you.

For the direct sales route, investment in equipment may be required. These requirements might include, as well as the table / canopy, a mobile refrigerated unit and utensils if you need them. Transport requirements are generally far simpler than the more conventional routes to market and there are usually no intermediaries involved. In other words, you bring it all in your own car / van / bicycle!

Online sales have huge potential for food producers and this route has grown considerably in the past few years. Good examples of ecommerce or online food sales in Ireland and the UK include Wyldsson (**www.wyldsson.com**), James Whelan Butchers (**www.jameswhelanbutcher.com**) or Graze (**www.graze.com**).

I first came across online ordering for meal delivery services capitalising on the growth of the health, convenience and fitness trends in London a few years ago and it now has taken off in Ireland too. Examples include newcomers Simply Fit Food (**www.simplyfitfood.com**), as well as established services like Bia At Home (**www.biaathome.ie**) in Ireland, or Hello Fresh (**www.hellofresh.com**) in the UK, both of which deliver full meals. There are many more all across the country, and not just in the cities.

There are costs associated with online sales, with website design and maintenance to be considered. Nonetheless, some producers *only* sell online, while other producers provide an ordering service by telephone.

Delivery of orders from online or telephone sales could be managed on a rotation basis by a group of producers in a local area. An example of this is the Irish Food Co-op based in Kilkenny (find them on Facebook). However, unless one person takes control of the managing orders and organising the deliveries, this rarely works out and most producers just arrange or deliver all their own produce themselves. Alternatively, the consumer might collect their order either from the producer, farm-gate / house / shop, or from a central distribution point.

More recently, online shops have been set up which producers can use to help get their foods to market. Examples of these are **www.indiefude.com** and FixItFood (**www.fixitfood.com**) and Larder 360 (**www.larder360.com**). There are plenty of examples in the UK, such as **www.localfooddirect.co.uk,   www.bigbarn.co.uk** and **www.farmdrop.com**.

Shows / Events / Concerts are a great way to get your food produce to your customers. There are many annual Christmas markets and fairs around the country, food festivals, Bloom in the Park, agricultural and County Shows and so on. These provide a chance for consumers to try out new products, and for producers to test the market without having to make a longer-term commitment to a market, week in week out.

Other **Direct Routes** include:

- **Weddings:** If you plan to make products for the wedding market, then it's wedding fairs you should target, as well as shops selling wedding dresses, suit hire, florists or anything associated with the event – and don't forget hen parties!

- **Celebrations:** If you plan to make celebration cakes for birthdays, first holy communions, christenings, bar / bat mitzvahs or other family occasions, then leave cards or flyers in children's play centres, clothes shops, babywear and baby equipment shops and so on.

The direct route to market is labour-intensive and requires good organisation and management, and a strong commitment from producers who are willing to travel and manage orders and deliveries.

Indirect Sales

Route to market options for indirect sales include the following:

- **Multiples:**
  - *SuperValu* and *Centra* stores are supplied through the Musgrave Chilled Distribution System. However, individual shops in this supermarket group also purchase directly from local suppliers. SuperValu and Bord Bia run the *Food Academy* through the Local Enterprise Offices, which gives successful participants ready access to a number of local SuperValu stores with a view to gaining national sales in the longer term. Contact your LEO for details (**supervalu.ie/real-people/food-academy-programme**);
  - Producers who want to sell in *Tesco* must make their approach *via* head office in Dublin, not to local stores (**www.tescoplc.com/contacts/suppliers/**). The Tesco Taste Bud programme (**www.tesco.ie/tastebud**) is an annual seven-month programme that supports participants to develop the necessary skills required to secure, grow and maintain a listing with Tesco in Ireland and overseas;
  - *Lidl's* Taste of Success programme on RTE television (**www.lidl.ie**) promotes food start-ups and Aldi runs a National Brown Bread baking competition (**www.aldi.ie/national-brown-bread-baking-competition**) in association with the National Ploughing Championships (**www.npa.ie**) and the Irish Countrywomen's Association (**www.ica.ie**) – the winner is stocked in stores for 12 months;
  - *Dunnes Stores' Simply Better* range promotes local producers and names them on the label, as well as sponsoring the Small Producer of the Year award as part of this year's Irish Quality Food and Drink Awards – open to food producers

and manufacturers across the Republic of Ireland and
Northern Ireland (**www.dunnesstores.com**);

- o Bord Bia has a development programme for Irish producers
  wanting to get into the UK. Check out its *Guide to Retail for
  Small Food Producers*, which has some useful tips though no
  contact details;

- o You also could exhibit at the annual Speciality Food Fair in
  London (**www.specialityandfinefoodfairs.co.uk**) and try to
  meet supermarket buyers in the UK that way. There is more
  about how to prepare for meeting supermarket buyers below;

- **Distributors, Agents and Wholesalers:** You might decide that
  using a third party to bring your foods to the shops and consumers
  is a good option. These come in all sorts of shapes and sizes. Some
  market stall holders will sell your foods for you, some agents will
  sell your foods to shops they have on their route, some wholesalers
  will buy from you and sell it on, some distributors will sell as well
  as deliver. Whichever of these, or combination of them, you go for,
  make sure you are happy for them to represent you and your
  foods. See more below;

- **Specialist shops:** Some butchers, baker or fruit and veg shops may
  be interested in discussing terms with local producers when a
  product is ready for supply, provided it does not compete with
  their own lines. In fact, it can be a good idea to explain to any shop
  owner that your products might bring in more customers, making
  it a win-win!

- **Food Service:** This is the term used to describe all food consumed
  outside the home – for example, catering, in restaurants, hotels,
  canteens, hospitals, schools, vending machines, pubs and so on. If
  you are able to make a quality product with your USPs clearly
  defined, then local restaurateurs, hotels, cafés and pubs who are
  motivated and interested in using and promoting local producers
  might be interested. Some restaurateurs are prepared to pay a
  premium, especially those who are interested in provenance and
  promoting local food. Be careful though, make sure you arrange
  for cash on delivery if you can, or at least don't allow credit to

build up. You might decide that your foods would sell well through these outlets and it is a growing sector, with more and more people eating on-the-go;

- **Independent retailers / artisan outlets:** It is always worth talking to local independent retailers who may take small quantities initially to test the local market and to get feedback. You might have to agree to a sale or return arrangement (where you only get paid if the food sells, and you have to take back anything that doesn't sell) – this is quite common, in fact. It's not a bad way to start since the shop owner is not taking on any risk and so may be more inclined to accommodate you.

Meet the Buyer

You've managed to get a face-to-face meeting and a chance to present your foods to a supermarket or food service buyer. Well done! These opportunities do not come easily or often, so you want to make the most of it.

So, in preparation, what do you need to consider? First, ask yourself what you hope to gain from this meeting. There are no guarantees, and you really want to put your best foot forward. Buyers see a lot of suppliers and producers so you'll want to stand out for all the right reasons!

Here are some tips:

- Be prepared, practice your spiel. Make a good impression – one that they will remember;
- Tell them about yourself, your background, how you came to set up your food business;
- Talk about your foods, why they're so good, their USPs;
- Bring samples in packaging and some to taste;
- Be clear about the finances and about your ability to supply;
- Come away with a name, contact details and clarity around next steps.

Knowing your costs cannot be emphasised enough. You must know what wriggle room you have when it comes to negotiating prices.

Many smaller shops will be happy to try your foods out on a sale or return basis to begin with. In other words, effectively they don't buy them from you, but take a cut on whatever is sold, and you take back whatever is unsold. The retailers are in business after all and need to minimise their risk. *Top Ten Tips for Meeting the Buyer* can be downloaded free from my website **www.alphaomega.ie.**

Distribution

Food distribution is generally a major obstacle for start-up producers. Unless you intend to drive around the country yourself (and you might have to in the beginning), then you will have to either hire a driver or find a distributor. Options include 'wheels only' couriers who pick up and drop off, while others offer merchandising where they will stock shop shelves for you (at a cost, of course). Food wholesalers and chilled foods distributors – such as Pallas (**www.pallasfoods.eu**), Crossgar Foodservice (**online.crossgar.ie**) or Musgrave Food Services (**foodservices.musgrave.ie**) and many others – offer a variety of services. Don't assume that just because you may be small that they won't be interested in you as a customer.

Other distributors also have expressed interest in new niche, high quality, artisan food products. Some examples include: Independent Irish Health Foods Ltd. (**www.iihealthfoods.com**); Brandshapers (**www.brandshapers.ie**); M&K Meats (**www.mkmeats.eu**); Wholefoods Wholesale (**www.wholefoods.ie**) and many others.

Get out the phone book, search the Internet, keep an eye on the lorries delivering to your local shop and approach the driver, talk to other producers for recommendations, and check out Bord Bia's Distributor search tool on **www.bordbia.ie** and its *Guide to Distribution for Food and Drink Producers in Ireland.*

Distribution comes at a cost, and so most producers do the distribution themselves initially. This is hard work, so you should try to plan your week and your route to be as efficient as possible. However, as your business grows, you will have to pay someone to do the driving, whether your employee or someone else, so you must build this cost into your price from the beginning. A rough rule of thumb is that distribution costs could be as much as 33% of the retail price.

Branding

Earlier, we talked about provenance and the importance of letting your customers know where your food is made. The next step is to promote this through your branding.

The Fuchsia brand of food, tourism and crafts in West Cork (**www.westcorkaplaceapart.com**), the Yorkshire Pantry (**www.theyorkshirepantry.com**), Taste of Scotland (**www.taste-of-scotland.com**) and Food NI (**www.nigoodfood.com**) are all good example of how regional branding has been used to promote a group of producers under one umbrella.

The Love Irish Food brand (**www.loveirishfood.ie**) is an umbrella brand for various Irish-based producers, large and small.

Branding is always aligned to quality. A strong brand provides familiarity and creates an expectation in the mind of your customer about the level of quality in the product. Familiar food brands have strong associations for people, such as Siúcra (even though no sugar is produced in Ireland anymore!), the old Quinnsworth Yellow Pack (perceived low quality) or the premium ranges from supermarkets' own brands (high quality).

Branding vs Labelling

What is the difference between branding and labelling? There are important differences between them. Food labelling is used to inform consumers of the properties of pre-packaged food, and the most important rule of labelling is that the consumer should not be misled (more about this in **Chapter 7**). A brand distinguishes your food from everyone else's. The brand conjures up an expectation in people's minds as to what your food will be like, where it comes from, who made it, how it's made, the ingredients, quality, and so on. While a label is functional and its main purpose is to provide specific information, a good label can enhance a brand also.

Logo

Differentiation is very important so that your customer recognises your food label easily or does not mix your foods up with someone else's, and buy their product by mistake. As you may have a number of similar competitors, it is essential that your brand has a clear, marked difference. The logo should be evident on your packaging, website, adverts, social media, your email signature, everywhere! Ideally, people should recognise it immediately.

Graphic designers might advise that you should be brave and make a real statement, by having something different rather than creating a 'me too' brand. For example, take a look at Ben & Jerry's ice cream branding. This brand was developed in the 1970s, and still looks fresh and full of personality today. Even Coca Cola has modified its logo over the years. Brave branding offers a real opportunity to create a mark of difference between yourself and your competitors. Dare to be different! Talk to your graphic designer, be clear about what your brand stands for, what your 'brand values' are, and work with them to come up with something original. A really good example of this is Velvet Cloud sheep's milk yogurt, which features as a Case Study in **Chapter 13.**

There are lots of graphic designers out there, get Googling or ask around. Take a look at their work to see if you like it, or are all their logos a bit same-y? I recently used **www.fiverr.com** for something cheap and cheerful that did the job I needed at the time.

Defining your brand

The provenance, USPs and product characteristics of your food should be captured in your brand. Areas to consider when developing your brand include:

- **Core brand values:** Functional, emotional, coherence, consistency, credibility, innovation, co-operation, belief, partnership;
- **Where you see the brand going:** Your plans for growth and adding more product lines / food varieties.

It is important to remember that every element reflects the brand, whether it is your packaging, press releases, personality or communication.

If sub-branding (a 'Lite' version of your product, for example) is needed, ensure that it enhances the brand. Sub-brands often can weaken and confuse an overall brand.

A strong brand can provide competitive advantage in the marketplace. Your competitors may be trading also on quality, local, and artisan issues. Competition from large suppliers to supermarkets has to be considered, too.

Brand recognition is the extent to which a brand is recognised for its stated brand attributes or communications. Consumers will make associations with certain brands, both good and bad. Your food will need to communicate its brand along with the provenance, USPs and logo in order to earn recognition. Consistency is important so that the customer recognises the brand across a range of foods. Cadbury's does this well, so does Danone – no matter that the product, their main logo appears on the advert or label somewhere.

In developing a brand strategy for your foods, consider this example for a new healthy convenience food:

- Establish and promote its credentials as a source of high quality, nutritious, flavoursome, ready to eat foods;
- Promote the brand through social media channels in advance of launch and continue throughout launch period;
- Position it as an important new enterprise development initiative;
- Use growing consumer recognition of the brand to stimulate ongoing product development;
- Develop marketing strategies to continually advance the brand;
- Develop distribution channels and both foodservice and retail market opportunities.

So how do you know if your strategy is working? You need to measure a few things, what you might call key performance indicators or targets. For example:

- The number of suppliers / providers for your new product;
- Sales volumes driving growth in its suppliers;
- Consumer recognition and awareness levels of the brand (you could do a survey);

- The number of new retail / foodservice / forecourt outlets secured;
- Profile of key accounts – what are sales like in the various outlets;
- Visibility of the brand in marketing initiatives undertaken in retailers.

Trade Marks

Trade marks are symbols (like logos and brand names) that distinguish goods and services in the marketplace. A trade mark must be distinctive for the goods and services you provide. In other words, it must be recognisable as a sign that differentiates your goods or service from someone else's. A trade mark is the means by which a business identifies its goods or services and distinguishes them from the goods and services supplied by other businesses.

A trade mark may consist of words (including personal names), designs, logos, letters, numerals or the shape of goods or of their packaging, or of other signs or indications that are capable of distinguishing the goods or services of one undertaking from those of others.

Examples of familiar international food trade marks are: Kerrygold, Fairtrade, Cadbury, Coca Cola, McDonalds. Make sure you don't use a registered trade mark, name or logo or it could get you into trouble!

Talk to the Patents Office (**www.patentsoffice.ie** or **www.gov.uk/browse/business/intellectual-property**) for more information.

Unique Selling Points

We've talked about this already, but honestly, you can't talk about it enough. Everyone can come up with several unique selling points (USPs) for their food, it just takes a bit of thought and effort. These USPs should be exploited in order to increase the value of your food to the trade and the consumer.

In order for the customer or consumer to be convinced to buy your food, then the USPs must be clear. A USP defines a product's competitive advantage and is essential to identify what makes your food different from your competitors. These advantages must be emphasised every time you talk about your food to anyone who will listen!

Provenance

For food businesses, it is really important that your provenance story is communicated well both on your packaging and through all other communication channels – website, social media, blog, advertising and images. Focusing on provenance and local sourcing provides food producers with an opportunity to differentiate themselves from competitors, especially large factory food producers. Food provenance is increasingly sought after by consumers, food writers and journalists, so talk it up!

A good example of a food business using provenance to their advantage is the Truly Irish Country Foods (**www.trulyirish.ie**) brand. Bord Bia promotes Ireland as the Food Island in international marketing campaigns – just look at the Bord Bia channel on YouTube. The whole of Italy and France is known for its food. The Kerrygold brand is known internationally and is associated with green fields, soft rain, grazing cows. The 'Taste of … wherever' phrase is widely used in Ireland, Scotland and Northern Ireland.

A food's provenance will continue to be important, in particular for locally-produced food. This may be driven in part by the expectation that local food is fresher, but also the trend continues for shoppers to be increasingly keen to support local producers if they can.

Consumer research has found that, when you ask them, most shoppers prefer to buy local food, mainly because they want to support the local economy. The overall findings indicated that consumer demand is for authenticity, with health, naturalness and freshness being the primary motivating factors for purchase.

In the UK, the *Guardian* newspaper has reported that, for every £1 spent with a small or medium-sized business, 63p stayed in the local economy, compared to 40p with a larger business.

So, the provenance relating to your food products needs to be clearly defined. Take a look at some tourism websites for vocabulary: some of them are great at describing lush heathery mountainsides, sea spray, wild landscape and all that good stuff! A word of warning though – you can have all the provenance, Granny's recipe, three generations of farmers and whatever you like … but if your food doesn't taste good, if it's not good quality, they'll not be back.

Food Tourism

Some places are great at attracting tourists – castles, mountains, sea, sports, walking, cycling, culture, music – you name it, they all entice tourists to an area. Food can be used to great effect too, with food trails, food-themed events, food experiences, good restaurants, food markets, local producers and so on being reason enough for some people (like me!) to visit. If you can tie your food business in with these, then you can piggy-back on their marketing activities.

In Northern Ireland, food tourism is worth over £350 million annually to the local economy. In the Republic of Ireland, it's in the order of €2 billion!

Take the Greenway Cycleway in Co. Mayo in the West of Ireland – the Gourmet Greenway quickly appeared alongside it, with food producers, tearooms, restaurants and gastro pubs all letting the tourists know that they are nearby. The Wild Atlantic Way is another – with books published in no time at all listing all the foodie places along the way.

Marketing

Marketing is the assessment, creation and meeting of demand. The more detailed the market research, the sounder, more reliable the rest of your business planning will be.

You might have heard about something called the 'marketing mix', also known as the 'four Ps': Product, Place, Price and Promotion. Sometimes three more Ps are added: Process, Physical Evidence and People. All of these go towards developing your approach to marketing. So many producers I know overlook the importance of planning for marketing activities, and don't budget for them. You really must do both – plan *and* budget.

When you write your marketing plan, it usually looks at all the things we've talked about in the previous chapters, and pulls them together, including:

- **Business profile:**
  - Organisational structure – who does what, who is in charge;
  - Description of your range of foods or drinks;
- **Situation analysis:**
  - Internal Factors – Strengths, Weaknesses, Opportunities and Threats (SWOT analysis);
  - External Factors – Political, Economic, Social, Technological, Legislative and Environmental (PESTLE analysis);
  - Consumer trends;
  - Competitors;
- **Market segmentation:**
  - Target market;
  - Consumer analysis;
  - Market size;
  - Route to market – different routes will need different approaches;
  - Demographics;
- **Marketing objectives**
  - Market share objectives – what % of the market are you after?
  - Profit objectives – what profit level are you looking for?;
  - Increasing brand awareness;
- **Marketing communications:**
  - Exhibitions, consumer food fairs and events, trade shows;
  - Awards and competitions you plan to enter (see below);
- **Promotions:**
  - Objectives – more shops, more sales (always!);
  - Activities – campaigns, offers, meetings and so on;

> o   Examples: Buy One, Get One Free (BOGOF), Multi-buys (3 for 2), Extra % free, on pack offers, in-store tastings (retailers LOVE these!), in-store recipe leaflets, social media campaigns….

We will not consider marketing any further here, since it's a huge topic in its own right, but you really must recognise its importance and look out for training courses or marketing mentors in your area to help you if necessary.

I will give you two tips though:

- Put together a marketing calendar – a list of marketing activities and when you will do them, how much they will cost you (you must put aside some money for marketing);
- Promotions planning – when you will put foods on special offer.

I've put examples of both of these as free downloads on **www.alphaomega.ie.**

Social Media Marketing

Social media is an everyday part of business now. It's not an extra, it's not something you do if you have time, it's not just for fun, friends or family. It's essential. Not spending time on social media or digital marketing as part of your marketing activities, or maybe as your only marketing activity, is akin to saying in the 1940s that television was a fad and would never take off!

Facebook, Twitter, Vimeo, YouTube and the rest are all free to use, other than the cost of your time. There is a charge if you take out adverts on the various platforms, but you don't have to. Compared to other media, it's a cheap and effective way to spread the word about your business, your new products, your provenance and your brand – everything you want to tell the world about your food. If you feel it's not for you, if you don't have time or skills, then either get someone to do it for you or get some training, but don't ignore it.

You should register your business on your chosen social media channel as soon as you can, as many names are already taken. Check out **www.namecheck.com** to see if yours is available.

If you need help getting to grips with social media, then contact your Local Enterprise Office, they're always running courses on Facebook for Business and the like. I've listed some books in **Chapter 16**.

Food Awards and Competitions

Entering your food product into any of the many food awards and competitions is a great way to get free promotion and PR for you and your food business. The big ones in Ireland are the Blas na hÉireann Awards and the IQFAs (Irish Quality Food Awards). In the UK, it's the Great Taste Awards and the Quality Food Awards. So, you should definitely take a look at them:

- Blas na hÉireann Awards / National Irish Food Awards (**www.irishfoodawards.com**);
- Food Quality Awards (UK) (**www.qualityfoodawards.com**);
- Good Food Ireland (**www.goodfoodireland.ie**);
- Great Taste Awards (UK) (**http://greattasteawards.co.uk**);
- Irish Quality Food and Drink Awards (**www.irish.qualityfoodawards.com**).

There is also an annual award from the Irish Food Writers Guild, details of which can be found at **www.irishfoodwritersguild.ie**. Euro-toques also has awards, with details of past winners available on **www.euro-toques.ie**. Local Enterprise Offices have county and national awards competitions too, so does the Small Firms Association (**www.sfa.ie**), and the banks all sponsor awards too and there are many others.

If you get shortlisted, even if you don't win, it's great for your profile and it's all free advertising!

7

LABELLING, NUTRITION CLAIMS AND ALLERGENS

Food Labelling

Food labelling is used to tell consumers what is in their food. If your food is in a packet, bag, carton, jar or bottle when it leaves your kitchen (**pre-packed**), then it must have a label on it. Generally, if food is sold loose, like in a bakery, or deli counter or market stall and you only put it into a bag when you're handing it over to the customer, then it doesn't need a label.

However, new legislation also applies to **unwrapped** or **non-prepacked** foods in relation to allergens. It requires all food businesses including restaurants, delis, canteens, pubs, takeaways and retail outlets providing non-prepacked foods, such as unwrapped foods or meals, to indicate to consumers the use of any of the 14 listed allergenic ingredients in the production or preparation of the food. We talk more about allergens below.

The most important rule of labelling is that the consumer should not be misled. The label cannot make any claims about a food's ability to prevent, treat or cure a human illness – snake-oil salesmen take note!

'Labelling' means any words, trade marks, brand name, pictures or symbols relating to the food and placed anywhere relating to the food. The information on the label must be easy to understand, be clearly legible, it must also be indelible, easy-to-see and not obscured in any way. Food products, including food imports sold in Ireland, must be labelled in English (with optional labelling in Irish as well as, but not instead of, English).

There is specific additional labelling legislation for:

- Meat from pigs, sheep, goats, poultry;
- Beef;
- County of Origin for honey, olive oil, fruit and vegetables, fish;
- Products with meat as an ingredient;
- Jams, jellies and marmalades (see **Chapter 11**);
- Foods containing quinine or caffeine;
- Food supplements;
- Alcoholic beverages;
- Additives.

Some of these are covered below. For the others, ask your EHO, for example, or look them up on **www.fsai.ie**, **www.food.gov.uk** or **www.foodstandards.gov.scot** or read *EU Regulation 1169/2011*.

There is an exception to the rule for small packages or containers where the largest surface is less than $10cm^2$ (such as chocolate wedding favours) – in this case, only the name of the food, the net quantity, date of minimum durability and any allergens, (for example, the words 'contains peanuts') are required.

There are now requirements about the minimum font size, which specifies a font size where the x-height is equal to or greater than 1.2mm (your graphic designer will know what this means). And, in the case of packaging or containers, the largest surface of which has an area of less than $80cm^2$, the x-height of the font size must be equal to or greater than 0.9mm.

What Must Appear on the Label?

There is a mountain of legislation about food labelling. However, you should start with general labelling legislation, which says that the following must appear on the label:

1. Name of the food;
2. List of ingredients;

3.   Allergens;

4.   Quantity of certain ingredients;

5.   Net quantity;

6.   Date of minimum durability –Best Before or Use By dates;

7.   Special storage instructions or conditions of use;

8.   Name or business name and address of the producer, manufacturer, packager, seller or importer within the EU;

9.   Country of Origin or Place of Provenance (see above);

10. Instructions for use, if necessary;

11. Beverages with more than 1.2% alcohol by volume must declare their actual alcoholic strength;

12. Nutrition Declaration.

There are many exceptions and special cases for all elements of the labelling legislation. What is described here is for food in general. For any specifics relating to *your* food, it's a good idea to check your labels with your EHO / Inspector.

Name of the Food

This means its legal name, such as 'chocolate' or 'butter' or otherwise its customary name, say 'shepherd's pie' or 'fish fingers' or the name that describes what it actually is, like 'vegetable soup'. If you call your product something vague like 'Mary's Winter Casserole', then you'd have to add a line so that customers know exactly what it is.

So, this element of your label might look like:

Mary's Winter Casserole
Beef and vegetables in gravy

List of Ingredients

The ingredients should be listed in descending order of quantity, starting with the ingredient with the largest amount in your recipe. In addition:

- Products requiring reconstitution may be listed as dehydrated or rehydrated;

- If you use additives, then you can either use the E number alone or the name, or both, as you prefer – for example, 'thickener (E412)', 'thickener (Guar Gum)' or 'thickener (E412/Guar Gum)';

- For compound ingredients (ingredients that have more than one component themselves, such as the pastry in a fruit pie or mayonnaise in coleslaw), you must list their ingredients separately too unless they are less than 2% of the final product – and there are some other exceptions;

- The amount of added water need not be listed as an ingredient if it is less than 5% by weight of the finished product;

- If you are using water for ingredient reconstitution (in other words, using it to reconstitute dry ingredients before adding them into your sausage mixture, for example) or if the water is not going to be eaten (like tuna or olives in brine), then you do not have to declare it as an ingredient;

- If your food contains certain allergens (ingredients that are scientifically proven to cause an allergic reaction), then you must highlight them within the ingredients list, see below.

Allergens

The way that certain allergens are required to be listed on labels is described specifically in the legislation (see *Annex II of Directive EU 1169/2011*).

INGREDIENTS
Water, Carrots, Onions, Red Lentils (4.5%) Potatoes, Cauliflower, Leeks, Peas, Cornflower, **Wheat**flour, Cream (**milk**), Yeast Extract, Concentrated Tomato Paste, Garlic, Sugar, **Celery** Seed, Sunflower Oil, Herb and Spice, White Pepper, Parsley
ALLERGY ADVICE
For allergens, see ingredients in **bold**

© http://www.foodlabel.org.uk/label/allergens.aspx

The allergens that must be listed are:

1. Cereals containing gluten, namely: wheat (such as spelt and khorasan wheat), rye, barley and oats – *allergen* here means the name of the cereal – for example, 'wheat' and not 'gluten';

2. Crustaceans (crabs, lobsters, crayfish, shrimp);

3. Eggs;

4. Fish;

5. Peanuts;

6. Soybeans;

7. Milk;

8. Nuts, namely: almonds, hazelnuts, walnuts, cashews, pecan nuts, Brazil nuts, pistachio nuts, macadamia or Queensland nuts – *allergen* here means the name of the nut – for example, 'pistachio nut' and not 'nut';

9. Celery;

10. Mustard;

11. Sesame seeds;

12. Sulphur dioxide and sulphites at concentrations of more than 10 mg/kg or 10mg/L;

13. Lupin (lupin flour or lupin seeds can be used in baking);

14. Molluscs (snails, clams, oysters, octopus, squid);

That's quite a list! So, if you are unsure, ask for help from your EHO or Inspector or other qualified nutrition or food science and technology expert or from the FSAI, FSA or Food Standards Scotland, as appropriate.

Quantity of Certain Ingredients
This is called QUID, short for 'quantitative ingredient declaration'. What it means is that, in certain instances, the percentage of specific ingredients is declared on a label if the name of the food implies that the food contains a specific ingredient – for example:

• Pineapple yogurt – declare the percentage of pineapple;

• Irish Stew – declare the percentage of lamb;

• Chilli con Carne – declare the percentage of beef;

• "with cheesy topping" – declare the percentage of cheese;

• Leek and Potato Soup – declare the % leek and % potato.

The first image below is the back panel from a sachet of Italian tomato pasta sauce. The ingredients list must declare the various ingredients mentioned in its name. In this case, the percentage of tomatoes and tomato purée are given.

RECIPE INGREDIENTS
Tomatoes (51 %), Onions, Olive Oil, Tomato Pureé (4 %), Sugar, Peppers, White Wine Vinegar, Spring Onions, Chillies, Sea Salt, Cracked Black Pepper, Garlic.

Greek style chickpea and sesame seed paste dip with lemon juice and garlic

Ingredients
Cooked Chickpeas (43%) [Chickpeas, Water], Rapeseed Oil, **Sesame** Seed Paste (16%), Water, Concentrated Lemon Juice (3%), Garlic Purée, Salt, Preservative (Potassium Sorbate).
Allergy Advice: For allergens, see **highlighted** ingredients. Manufactured in a plant that handles Egg, Milk, Gluten, Crustaceans, Soya Bean, Mustard, and Fish.

Photos: Anna Quinn

The second image relates to a tub of hummus, whose legal name is 'Greek-style chickpea and sesame seed paste dip with lemon juice and garlic'. Since the consumer expects hummus to contain chickpeas among other things, the ingredients list must declare the percentage of these used. It was considered unnecessary to declare the percentage of the various types of nuts.

QUID is not required if the percentage declaration is covered by other legislation, like in the case of jam (see below). However, you might like to declare all the vegetable percentages if you are producing a mixed vegetable soup, for example, because it's a good way of showing your customers all the tasty ingredients that are in it!

Net Quantity

The net quantity means the weight of the food without its packaging. Some products are exempt from weight marking, such as herb packs weighing less than 5g, or sugar confectionery of less than 50g. In 1981, Ireland introduced the average system of weight control denoted by the **'e'** mark. What this means in effect is that the weight of the food is an average weight.

For example, let's say your pre-packed bag of buns has a stated weight on the label of 250g. Then if you weighed 10 bags of buns, on average, each bag would have to weigh 250g, even if some were a little bit more and some a little bit less. If you want to start getting into the complexities as to how much a 'little bit' actually means, you can check out the legislation in detail (*EC Packaged Goods (Quantity Control) Act, 1980* and *Packaged Goods (Quantity Control) Act, 1981*).

Date of Minimum Durability – Best Before or Use By dates

The difference between Best Before and Use By dates was covered in the Shelf Life section of **Chapter 5**. As described by SafeFood (**www.safefood.eu**), Best Before is a *guideline* and Use By is a *deadline*.

The key difference is that Use By is for perishable foods that might cause food poisoning or illness, because they are likely to contain unacceptable levels of bacteria or other microbes after that date.

Generally, foods that must be kept in the fridge to maintain their safety rather than their quality, and that have a relatively short shelf life after they have been made, require a Use By date – for example, ready-to-eat foods or foods that must be cooked or reheated before eating, such as meat, fish, poultry, and eggs as well as some dairy products.

Frozen foods have a *Best Before* date. Again, there are some exceptions, so check out what's right for your food.

Special Storage Instructions and/or Conditions of Use

If the food must be kept in the fridge or in a cool dry place in order to maintain its shelf life, then you need to put this message on the label to tell the consumer what they have to do when they get the food home.

You also should mention how long to keep the pack once opened, or whether they need to store it in the fridge once opened.

Name or business name and address of the food business
(manufacturer, packager, seller or importer)
The contact details must be precise enough so that, in the event of a customer complaint, the complainant can contact you. You should use a postal address, somewhere a letter can reach you. A website address or phone number is not acceptable on their own. It is very important to note that, even if you outsource your production to someone else (a third party), it is YOUR name and address that should be on the label, not theirs.

Country of Origin or Place of Provenance
Some foods must provide country of origin information (fruit and vegetables, honey, olive oil, fish). Beef, pigmeat, sheepmeat, goat and poultry products must have details of where the animal was born, reared and slaughtered.

For some other foods, the place of provenance is required if its absence might mislead the consumer to a material degree – you only need to do something about this if, for example, you make 'Italian sausage', but you make it in Cork, or you make Brie cheese (typically a French cheese) in Tipperary. It needs to be clear on the label where the food was made. As long as the consumer doesn't think it came from some place it didn't, then that's fine.

Instructions for Use
This is where you tell the customer how to prepare, cook or reheat the food, whether it's suitable for frying or baking, or whether it should be thawed before use, for example.

Alcoholic drinks
Beverages with more than 1.2% alcohol by volume must declare their actual alcoholic strength.

Nutrition Labelling

When you read a label and see a table that lists the Energy (kJ or Cal), Fat, Carbohydrate, Protein, and Salt in the product, this is called 'nutrition labelling'. Since December 2016, nutrition information has become mandatory for most pre-packaged foods. There are some exemptions for food producers making small quantities (defined as 250 kg or litres of products per week, or 13,000 kg or litres of products per year, or 500 units per week, or 26,000 units per year) of products to the final consumer or to local (<100km away from where you're making it) retail establishments.

However, even before it became a legal requirement, many producers chose to label their foods with nutrition information to enable consumers to make more informed choices about the nutrition characteristics of the food. It costs money to analyse and list the various nutrients, and to print up the labels, so don't do this until you are sure that you won't be changing the recipe any time soon.

So how do you work out the nutritional analysis figures? There are three ways:

- Send the food off to a lab for analysis;
- Work it out by hand using your recipe and the tables of figures for the various ingredients from McCance and Widdowson's book, *The Composition of Foods*;
- Use special nutritional analysis software to work it out (NutriCalc, MicroDiet or NutritionalPro are some examples).

Any of these methods is acceptable. The second option is laborious, and it depends on how much you like getting stuck into calculations and formulae. You might find it cheaper to buy the software for a year than get your foods tested, depending on how many products you have to test. It is entirely up to you to choose the method.

The nutrients must be declared per 100g or per 100ml. The order in which they are listed is as follows (*and you must list them in this order*):

Mandatory Information / 100g or ml	Supplementary Information (if desired)
Energy (kJ / kcal)	
Fat of which Saturates	
	of which Monounsaturates of which Polyunsaturates
Carbohydrate of which Sugars	
	of which Polyols of which Starch
	Fibre
Protein	
Salt	
	Vitamins and Minerals (% RI)
You MUST list <u>all</u> of these.	**You MAY include all of these if you wish (either <u>all</u> or <u>none</u>).**

If you wish, you can add in another column to show the nutrition information *per portion*. For example, per biscuit, per bar, per sandwich. This is useful for the consumer who may find it tricky to work it out for themselves, but it's not a legal requirement.

Front of pack labelling is also voluntary – you can show the Energy on its own or the Energy, Fat, Saturates, Sugar and Salt (all of these).

Here's an example of a simple compliant label that you could give to a graphic designer:

Tomato and Basil Soup

Ingredients: Potato, Tomato (25%), Onion, Vegetable Stock, Basil (2%).

Use by: dd/mm/yyyy

Keep refrigerated. Once opened, use within 2 days.

Monnie's Fine Foods, Foodville, Co. Leitrim   e225g

Note that the following items must appear in the same field of vision on the label:

- Name;
- Net quantity;
- Actual alcohol content (if over 1.2% alcohol by volume).

Nutrition and Health Claims

If you claim that your food is high or low in fat or salt or calories or fibre, for example, then you have to be able to stand over this claim. The following are some examples of 'nutrition claims' that are defined in the legislation:

- **Reduced fat:** 30% reduction compared with standard product;
- **Low fat:** Maximum of 3g/100g per product;
- **Reduced calories:** 30% reduction compared with standard product;
- **Low calories:** Maximum 167Kj (40 Kcal) per product.

For more about nutrition claims, contact the FSAI or FSA.

The other type of claim that is sometimes made is a 'health claim' (covered under *Regulation (EC) 1924/2006*). This is any claim that states, suggests or implies that a relationship exists between a food (or one of its constituents) and health, such as reducing the risk of disease or referring to children's development and health (for example, "calcium is good for children's growth"). This is acceptable under law, *provided there is scientific data to prove it* (which can be difficult and expensive) or that the relationship has been around for so long that consumers understand it (for example, everyone knows that fibre is good for your digestion).

For example, the term 'probiotic', when used on a food label, is considered to be a health claim. However, there are no proven health claims registered with the EU at the moment and that includes probiotics.

Also, any health claim that states, suggests or implies that eating a particular food significantly reduces a risk factor in the development of human disease is prohibited! For more information check out **http://ec.europa.eu/nuhclaims/**.

Distance Selling

If you sell food over the Internet, the same labelling requirements apply as if you were selling it through a shop. Since the customer cannot examine the packaging before they purchase, since they can't hold it in their hand, then you must provide access to all of the mandatory food information *before* they complete their purchase. This mandatory information includes ALL information that must be given to the consumer, not just that on the label, and must be available before the purchase is concluded. The same goes for non-prepacked foods.

Organic Labelling

There are particular requirements for the labelling of organic products. In Ireland, information is available from one of two approved certification bodies:

- Irish Organic Farmers and Growers Association (**www.iofga.org**);
- Organic Trust (**www.organic-trust.org**).

There are nine certified organic bodies in the UK (including IOFGA and the Organic Trust) and you can find information about them **www.gov.uk/food-labelling-and-packaging/organic-food**.

Organic labelling includes requirements for displaying the organic certification license number, the symbol of the particular certification body with whom you are registered, as well as all the standard stuff above.

It is important to note that, just because the food is organic, you are not permitted to claim it is superior. If you use organic ingredients, then you can only apply for organic certification for your finished food if:

- Minimum of 95% by weight of total is certified organic material;
- Maximum of 5% by weight of total is from the permitted non-organically produced ingredient list.

Sometimes, you see labels declaring 'made using organic ingredients'. What this means usually is that, while the food producer themselves is not organic-certified, they buy organic-certified ingredients and use them in their foods.

Gluten-free labelling

Just because you use Tritamyl flour in your foods doesn't mean you can label them as being 'gluten-free'. By law, food labelled 'gluten-free' must contain less than 20mg gluten/kg (< 20 parts per million (ppm)). This level is suitable for the most sensitive of coeliacs. The specific legislation is *EU No 828/2014*, which you can look up on **http://eur-lex.europa.eu/homepage.html**.

So, if you bake bread and you want to label it as gluten-free, then you must be absolutely sure that it contains less than 20mg gluten/kg. It's not just a matter of complying with the legislation, but it could have a detrimental health implication for a person with coeliac disease if it doesn't. These are legal terms, not to be taken lightly!

'Wheat-free' does not mean that the product is gluten-free. The product may contain other gluten-containing cereals, such as spelt.

Sometimes you may see on a package 'Made in a factory handling gluten' or 'May contain gluten'. When you see this statement, the manufacturer has decided that there is a cross-contamination risk within the manufacturing process.

Crossed Grain Symbol European Licensing System

The Crossed Grain symbol is nationally and internationally recognised by those who need to follow a gluten-free diet as it is promoted by coeliac organisations worldwide. The symbol is synonymous with gluten-free and represents a sign of  safety and integrity. In an environment where food labels and legislative changes can be bewildering for someone on a gluten-free diet, the crossed grain symbol has been proven to provide consumers a quick reference point when out shopping and faced with the uncertainty on the gluten-free status of a product.

Source: www.coeliac.ie

To use the Crossed Grain symbol, your products must meet a range of criteria to ensure that they are gluten-free, both in terms of the ingredients and the production process. Obtaining a Crossed Grain licence for your product costs from €500 *pa*, depending on the turnover of your gluten-free products. The certification lasts for a full year from the date that the certification is taken out.

For details on licencing the Crossed Grain symbol or information on how you can better cater to the gluten-free consumer, contact the Coeliac Society of Ireland (**www.coeliac.ie**) or Coeliac UK (**www.coeliac.org.uk**).

Other Labels

Apart from the labelling requirements covered by legislation, what other labels might you put on your food?

Promotional labels like 'buy one, get one free', competition alerts to let the buyer know that they are in with a chance of winning something, awards labels shouting about your recent successes, flash labels to point out that your food is 'yeast-free' are some examples.

There is nothing from stopping you putting on any or all of these except that the legal labels have to take priority. Just be careful that it all doesn't get very crowded and unattractive-looking.

8

MAKING AND MANAGING MONEY

You don't necessarily need thousands of euros to start a small food business, though some people will need to invest in equipment and premises. The main thing in starting and maintaining a successful food business is a drive and a passion for what you are doing. However, you need to be sure that, having put in all the effort, you see some rewards, preferably monetary!

Pricing and Margins

When you hear people talking about pricing models and margins, what do they mean?

'Pricing' is what it actually costs you to make the product, plus a margin for your profit. Premium pricing is where your customer is willing to pay extra for something of special value to them. Consumers know that they usually get what they pay for, so cheap food implies poor quality and they expect to pay a bit more for artisan, good quality food.

'Margin' is the slice (or slices) that everyone in the supply chain takes – for example:

- The customer buys the food item for €4.00;
- That price includes the retailer's margin of €1.50;
- The distributor, who transfers the product from you to the retailer, charged 50c – which you have to pay before it is sold to the shop for €2.50;
- You (the producer) make the product for €2 total (including *everything!*).

It might seem to make sense to cut out the middlemen so that you, as the producer, can get the full retail price. When you are just starting out, you'll probably find that you have no choice here as you might not have the cash to pay a distributor. However, as you get busy, then you will find it more time- and cost-effective to have someone to distribute and sell your foods – even though this means you receive less revenue for each sale.

The difficulty is in knowing what margin a shop or supermarket will want; often this comes down to hard-nosed negotiations. The bigger supermarkets generally have a set margin they apply and you might not have much say in that. Smaller shops may operate on a sale or return basis, so you only get paid if the product is sold.

Regardless of where you sell, look at what your competitors are selling their products for and then you can work around that price as a starting point for cost / margin calculations.

Costs

The costs that you must consider include some or all of the following:

- Ingredients;
- Equipment (knives, scales, mincing equipment, cash till, etc.);
- Packaging;
- Training costs – food hygiene, social media, finance;
- Food safety costs, including the cost of aprons, gloves, hairnets, fridges, temperature probes, cloths, detergents, soaps, towels, waste containers and so on;
- Stall set-up costs, if you plan to sell at farmers' or country markets or at events / shows, including the stall itself, tables, canopies, banners, signs, etc.;
- Distribution costs – paying a distributor / courier / wholesaler or van driver;
- Vehicle costs, including a food trailer or refrigerated van if needed;
- Online selling costs, in addition to website development costs, domain registration;
- Returns – food that comes back unsold from the retailer.

Recipe Cost Calculation

CHOCOLATE CAKE	A Weight (g)	B Cost / weight used €
Butter	175	0.84
Chocolate	100	1.11
Flour	200	0.25
Baking powder	5	0.02
Bicarbonate of soda	5	0.02
Ground almonds	100	1.05
Dark brown sugar	275	1.60
3 Eggs (1 egg = 60g)	180	0.85
Buttermilk	150	0.12
ICING		
Chocolate	90	1.00
Butter	40	0.19
Double cream	150	0.95
INGREDIENTS COST		**8.00**
Electricity		0.50
Labour*		6.50
Packaging		2.00
TOTAL COST TO MAKE		**17.00**
Add on distribution costs		1.00
Add on margin		2.00
SELLING PRICE (direct sales)		**20.00**
Add on retailer's margin		5.00
SELLING PRICE (indirect sales)		**25.00**

*You must include payment for your labour. The majority of small food producers and indeed small businesses starting up forget this. But if you can't pay yourself, then you're not in business!

Now ask yourself: *Will a customer pay €25 for a chocolate cake?* The answer depends on why they are buying it. If it is a large cake for a special occasion, then the answer is probably, if not definitely, "Yes"!

As you get into the swing of your business, you may be able to source the same ingredients more cheaply. Or you may be able to substitute cheaper ingredients without compromising the quality.

Running Costs per day for a Food Stall

You should know your outlays before you even sell one loaf / jar / tub of anything at a market. Some markets charge more than others for the pitch, but this table will give you an idea of the costs.

		€
Rent of Stall	per day	25
Labour	8 hours / day / 1 person @ €10/hr	80
Insurance	Estimate per year (26 weeks)	40
Fuel	For travel to / from the market	5
TOTAL COST per day before you sell anything!		150

Projected Income

So how much are you hoping to earn? When I mentor new food businesses, I always suggest that they start with their aspirational income, whether it's replacing income from a current job or a target for where they want to get to.

So, let's say you want to earn €20,000 per year from baking chocolate cakes. In the example above, you're paying yourself €6.50 per cake, so that's 3,076 cakes per year you need to be selling! That's 10 cakes a day, six days a week!

Looking at it another way, if you want the business to turn over (in other words, bring in) €40,000 per year you need to make 2,222 cakes per year just to bring in €40,000 so that you can pay yourself €14,400.

If you want to pay yourself double that, or €28,800 per year, then charge more per cake, another €6.50 per cake in fact, but you'll still need to make over 2,000 cakes per year. Not really likely, is it?

My advice in this case would be to charge more per cake, let's say €40, and in that way you can increase your income and at the same time reduce the number of cakes you have to make.

Sources of Finance and Funding

The Local Enterprise Offices (LEOs) (**www.localenterprise.ie**), Local Authorities, County Councils and the Rural Development Partnerships (LEADER companies) (**www.nationalruralnetwork.ie**) or (**www.leader-programme.org.uk**) or Local Action Groups (UK) may have funding to help you with feasibility studies, training or equipment. In addition, they usually have a list of experienced mentors with specialisms in food, finance, business start-up and more that you can access, often for free, but certainly for a small percentage of the actual cost. The LEOs also may provide funding for attendance at trade shows.

Enterprise Ireland and Invest Northern Ireland have a great Innovation Vouchers scheme (**www.innovationvouchers.ie or www.investni.com**), which is open to food businesses that are registered companies. Sole traders are generally not eligible but sometimes the scheme is opened to sole traders or artisan producers, so keep an eye out for it. The New Frontiers programme (**www.enterprise-ireland.com**) is Ireland's national entrepreneur development programme, funded by Enterprise Ireland and delivered at a local level by the Institutes of Technology.

Inter*Trade*Ireland runs an annual SeedCorn competition for start-up and early stage businesses, as well as other funding for sales and marketing (Acumen programme) and for innovation (Fusion programme), once you're established and trading for a couple of years. The Elevate programme is a great way to develop cross-border sales across the island (**www.intertradeireland.com**).

The Food Works programme is a joint programme run by Bord Bia, Teagasc and Enterprise Ireland for new food start-ups (**www.foodworksireland.ie**). And check **www.bordbiavantage.ie** for more information on starting and marketing your food-based business.

There is a very useful website **www.supportingsmes.ie** where you can get a list of ALL the funding measures in the Republic of Ireland.

If you're looking for cash, try MicroFinance Ireland (**www.microfinanceireland.ie**) – and you can always try the banks!

You will need to write a business plan for many of the funding providers, while others have their own application forms. It's a good exercise to develop a business plan anyway as you'll get your ideas out of your head and onto paper – this will focus your mind and highlight any gaps in information you need to get.

My advice on funding – ask everyone! They will tell you quickly what is available and whether you're eligible or not. There are always new schemes, funding and training and mentoring programmes coming up. Don't assume anything – ask!

Insurance

I really advise that you should take out 'product liability' and 'public liability' insurance once you start selling your food. If you employ staff, then you'll need 'employer's liability' insurance too, and there may be other insurances to consider too, including 'product recall' insurance. Get advice from an insurance broker.

In Ireland, you can try IOMST, the Irish Organisation for Market and Street Traders (**www.iomst.ie**) or MAST, the Markets Alive Support Team (**www.mast.ie**), for insurance for market traders or. In the UK, try the Stallholders Club (**www.stallholders.org**) or Mobilers Insurance Services (**www.mobilers.co.uk**) – and there are many others.

Product liability insurance provides cover for you if you become legally liable to a member of the public for bodily injury/death/diseases and/or damages, expenses and costs as a result of a defective food product supplied by your or your company.

Public liability insurance is important if members of the public have access onto your property. It provides cover for you if you become legally liable to a member of the public for bodily injury/death/diseases, damages, expenses and costs and/or damage to their property following an accident, which is in connection with your business.

9

TRAINING REQUIREMENTS

As a food producer, you are required by law to have completed food hygiene instruction / training. While strictly speaking, you don't actually have to complete a course, most Inspectors prefer it if you have done one, and my advice is to do a one- or two-day Food Hygiene or Food Safety training course.

A good starting point if you want to find a trainer is to look online, in your local paper or ask another producer for a referral. The Environmental Health Association of Ireland (**www.ehai.ie**) lists all the registered trainers in the Republic of Ireland and upcoming courses. Both the FSAI and FSA has information on their websites that outline the requirements for you and your staff in relation to training, so take a look there first.

Some sector-specific training courses and providers are mentioned in **Chapters 12** to **15**; other, more general courses and providers are listed below. Contact details are provided in **Chapter 16**.

If you are working on your own, then you will need to have a really good understanding of HACCP also. There are courses available for this too, usually one or two days in duration. Some courses are available online.

Food Hygiene and Food Safety (HACCP)

Food safety training is essential in ensuring the preparation and service of safe food. It is a legal requirement that anyone involved in making foods, selling or distributing foods and working on food market stalls is adequately trained. You and your helpers (whether paid or unpaid) must have a knowledge and understanding of food hygiene and be able to demonstrate good hygiene practices. In addition, whoever is specifically involved in the design and implementation of the HACCP system must understand the principles of HACCP.

Regulation EC 852/2004, which covers the hygiene of foodstuffs, requires that food business operators (FBOs – that's you) must ensure:

- That food handlers are supervised and instructed and/or trained in food hygiene;
- That those responsible for the development and maintenance of HACCP have received adequate training in the application of the seven HACCP principles; and
- Everyone is trained in anything they're supposed to be trained in – ask your EHO / Inspector to find out what applies to your business.

Sticking strictly to good hygiene principles is really critical when you are making your food products. You are legally obliged to ensure your food is safe for consumption. Food hygiene and food safety training is essential in ensuring the preparation and service of safe food.

Some providers of food hygiene and safety training are listed in **Chapter 16** and include:

- About Hygiene Ltd;
- CAFRE (NI);
- Food Flow Training;
- Kennedy Food Technology;
- The Food Technology Centre at St. Angela's College, Sligo.

Most primary food hygiene trainers also deliver HACCP training. If you prefer to do your training in your own time, then there are also very many providers of food hygiene courses online.

After that, you can choose to do whatever training you like. Courses on everything from skills development (how to make cheese, etc.) to personal development to sales and marketing training are available around the country.

Finance / VAT training

When it comes to managing finances, it is a very good idea to do a short course, whether a one-day /evening course or as part of a Start your Own Business course, to help you keep on top of things. You must keep track of your costs, expenses and sales. If you find yourself working very hard, selling tons of product and yet are left with no money for shoes at the end of the year, then there is something wrong somewhere. Either you're undercharging, or your costs are too high, or both.

Sometimes, you can get free training through the LEOs depending on your circumstances.

Other Training

Ask your Local Enterprise Office or Council for information about courses for small businesses generally. Other food skills training providers include:

- CAFRE at Loughry College in NI has lots of courses, everything from cheese-making to train the trainer and more (**www.cafre.ac.uk**);
- National Organic Training Skillnet (NOTS) (open to non-organic producers also) (**www.nots.ie**);
- Taste 4 Success Skillnet (**www.taste4success.ie**);
- Teagasc (**www.teagasc.ie**);
- The Food Technology Centre, St. Angela's College, Sligo: Food labelling and legislation, sensory analysis techniques, product development and more) (**www.thefoodtechnologycentre.ie**);
- The Organic Centre (**www.theorganiccentre.ie**), Co. Leitrim.

You might consider taking a course in:
- Packaging techniques;
- Product labelling and legislation;
- Sales and marketing;
- Financial management for the small producer / business;
- Social media skills training (Facebook for Business, Twitter, etc.);
- IT skills development;

- Personal development/confidence-building;
- Product development, creativity and innovation;
- Sector skills – baking, sausage- and cheese-making, jam making, yogurt and ice cream courses;

and there are many more.

The FSAI has some free online courses in Labelling, Microbiological Criteria, Food Contact Materials and others. The Food Standards Agency has a really good e-learning programme for food labelling (**http://labellingtraining.food.gov.uk**).

10

BREAD AND BAKING

Opportunity

Most people I talk to who are considering starting up a food business at home are thinking about baking bread – usually brown bread. If not bread, then cakes, or buns. There are not as many apple-tart bakers!

While bread is an easy food to produce at home, you must ask yourself this first: is there really an opening for yet another bread baker? What could I bake that's a little different? Perhaps you should consider using spelt flour or rice flour, adding seeds or going after the health food or 'free from ...' market, or trying sourdough.

A great selling point can be to tell your prospective customers what your food does *not* contain! You might think people would know that traditional brown bread or soda bread is not made with yeast. But, why make assumptions? It's always good to point these things out to shoppers; it will catch their eye that way (a flashy sticker can be good here) and help you make sales.

So, try to do something a little different from the usual. The cupcake craze has probably reached its peak. It has had a good run, in fairness! Check out what's available, and try to fill a gap.

Most bread, cakes and fruit pies will sell all year round, even if only at weekends. There also will be increased demand around traditional family events – these offer big business opportunities for the local dessert maker or caterer, especially now when the trend is to entertain the family at home rather than in a hotel or restaurant. You could put up a notice in your local shop.

There are broadly two different categories of breads, depending on the raising agent you use: soda bread (traditional Irish) and yeast bread. Some people may have heard about the Chorleywood bread process, which is a high-volume process of making dough. The method was developed in 1961 by the British Baking Industries Research Association based at Chorleywood in England, and is now used to make the majority of white sliced pans. Compared to the traditional bulk fermentation process, the CBP, as it is called, is able to produce bread in a shorter time. The quality suffers, though, in many people's opinion. Home-producers of yeast bread or sourdough will be competing with the mass-producers. You can't complete on volume or price, but you can complete on quality, flavour, style and craft.

Ingredients and Production Requirements

The ingredients are simple: flour, salt, sugar (maybe treacle instead of sugar), seeds perhaps, yeast possibly ... there is no absolute list of ingredients for bread. And you can add almost anything to it to make it different. Push sprigs of rosemary into focaccia bread before baking, or chop up fresh rosemary and add it with freshly ground black pepper to plain white soda bread, or add cheese and onions or sundried tomatoes to scone mix. Get as fancy as you like or keep it simple. The possibilities are endless.

What You Need
You need:
- Suitable, approved premises;
- A bowl for mixing – plastic, ceramic, whatever you like;
- A clean, smooth surface for rolling-out and cutting;
- An oven;
- A place you can leave the bread to cool;
- A room to store the baked result.

You could decide to buy a bread-maker – a machine that takes a lot of the chore out of the process. To see which machine to buy, look at

www.bestbreadmachinereviews.com. Or you might prefer to stick with the truly hand-made method, elbow grease and all.

For packaging, you'll need tins, boxes, paper bags, plastic bags, foil trays, foil/paper inserts and trays for transporting the finished breads.

Set-up Costs
Set-up costs include the price of the equipment, although your own domestic oven, bowls and tins may suffice to begin with.

Running Costs
The main running costs involved are ingredients, electricity and labour. Unless you plan to wrap the bread, you won't need any packaging or labels. As with everything else we have talked about, don't forget to include your own time into any cost calculations. The cost of marketing and distribution is also extra.

Return on Investment
The price at which you can sell your bread / buns / scones / cakes will probably be higher than commercially-produced varieties – consumers expect to pay more for hand-made, home-produced baked goods, provided the quality and taste are there. Check local shops and see what other similar goods are being sold for. Maybe you'll only sell cupcakes or desserts at weekends. Most shops will have a sale or return policy for baked goods, so you will have to take home what doesn't sell ('returns') at your own cost. Go easy initially with the volumes! Keep an eye out for which varieties sell and which don't – and don't forget that there will be seasonal demand too.

Gluten-free
'Gluten-free' produce has experienced a huge increase in demand. Are there suddenly more people out there suffering from coeliac disease? Not according to the Coeliac Society! In Ireland and the UK, 1 in 100 people have been diagnosed with coeliac disease. But many other people find that they can't tolerate wheat very well, while others simply don't eat wheat through choice. In the past, good quality gluten-

free bread was hard to come by. However, improvements in baking techniques and the availability of gluten-free and other types of flour (rice, potato, etc.) have meant that good quality gluten-free breads are more readily available. By the way, spelt flour is not gluten-free!

While most people do not have coeliac disease and choose gluten-free for personal reasons, you should still work to a high standard so that if you say 'gluten-free' *on* the pack then it is gluten-free *in* the pack for this latter group of consumers. The labelling requirements for proper 'gluten-free' food suitable for coeliacs were discussed in **Chapter 7.**

Contamination during the baking process is a major hazard in a kitchen since your 'gluten-free' food can easily be contaminated with gluten from your other foods. Control here is critical and you really must get advice from your EHO or Inspector and from the Coeliac Society (**www.coeliac.ie** or **www.coeliac.org.uk**) about your set-up. The Coeliac Society's Food List team works with producers to make sure they comply with the standards for gluten-free foods and that no cross-contamination occurs during the manufacturing process.

To be absolutely sure that there is no cross-contamination, you will need a separate kitchen for your gluten-free products aimed at the coeliac market; this usually means a separate building. You'll also need:

- Dedicated equipment and utensils;
- Very high standards for cleaning;
- A very well-organised kitchen or bakery.

So how do you manage to control this? Why, through your HACCP system, of course (see **Chapter 3**)!

In order for products to be 'gluten-free' when they reach the consumer, you have to be absolutely sure that your baking process is tightly managed to prevent any contamination with gluten. Cross-contamination is the process by which a 'gluten-free' product loses that status because it comes into contact with something that is not 'gluten-free'.

Unless you are specifically aiming your foods at people with coeliac disease, when absolute certainty is paramount with regards to preventing cross-contamination, then one way to manage this is to make 'gluten-free' products at the start of the production day when contamination from dust is at a minimum and all equipment and clothing are thoroughly clean. Then follow 'gluten-free' products with gluten-containing products before cleaning. Alternatively, you could make your gluten-containing products on separate days from your 'gluten-free' products, with a thorough cleaning in between.

FSAI has a very detailed guidance note on its website (**www.fsai.ie**) about producing foods that are gluten-free.

Here's some of the many gluten-free producers now operating across the country:

- Bfree Foods (Dublin), **www.bfreefoods.com**;
- Check out My Buns (Belfast), **www.checkoutmybuns.com**;
- Denise's Delicious (Cork), **www.delicious.ie**;
- Goodness Grains (Longford), **www.goodnessgrains.com**;
- Honest Bakery (Roscommon), **www.honestbakery.ie**;
- Pure Bred (Donegal), **www.purebred.co.uk**;
- Rosaleen's Kitchen (Westmeath), **www.facebook.com/pg/rosaleenskitchens**.
- The Foods of Athenry (Galway), **www.thefoodsofathenry.ie**;

Current Trends and Future Developments

Spelt flour, rice flour, sour dough, rye ... never has there been such a variety of baked goods on the market. Some will come and go. Some will peak, be trendy for a while and then fall back to a reasonable everyday level (you know who you are, cupcakes!). While some foods will always be a regular part of the grocery basket, some are seen as treats and luxuries and so these will be purchased less often. Your food will compete for sales against all varieties of baked goods, so keep an eye out for what the consumers are looking for. The health food market is a big one. The influx of Polish immigrants in recent years has meant that Polish bakers have started baking selling their breads widely, and indeed these are being sold in supermarkets as well as in Polish shops.

Case Studies

Hillcrest Home Bakery

Hillcrest Home Bakery was established in May 2000 in Co. Mayo by four women, following the closure of the local bakery where they had all worked. Initially, Hillcrest made two products, a 9″ apple tart and a 9″ rhubarb tart. Since then its range has increased, with a great selection of confectionaries, including fruit and brown scones, ginger and treacle bread, rock buns and much more.

The co-founders of Hillcrest Home Bakery Ltd – Attracta Duffy, Angela Hession, Mary Higgins Molloy and Patricia Anderson – all take an active role in managing and working the business, with each having experience of working in various departments of the confectionary sector.

The business is built on a tradition of good quality baked products, produced to the highest quality, using a rich shortcrust pastry and the apple and rhubarb tarts are filled with a high fruit content. All the products are handmade and home baked, literally, in a unit behind the house of one of the ladies! You can find Hillcrest Bakery's tarts and cakes in supermarkets across the West of Ireland.

The Goodness Grains Bakery

The Kelleher Family has a long tradition in the service industry. One day in 2010 a customer asked Michael Kelleher for gluten-free bread to go with his lunch. Michael didn't have any but listened to what the customer had to say (and allowed him to use his own gluten-free bread which he carried around with him!) and the following day Michael had gluten-free bread on the menu!

Customers said that they found it extremely difficult to source fresh gluten-free products that have all the taste and choice of conventional foods. Given this feedback from customers, the Kellehers began to develop gluten-free products over a three-year period, and so Goodness Grains (**www.goodnessgrains.com**) opened in Longford in 2013 to bring quality fresh gluten-free products to the coeliac consumer in Ireland and increasingly also to non-coeliacs choosing a gluten-free diet.

The bakery is one of the very few purpose-built gluten-free bakeries in the country. Goodness Grains is the only company in Ireland and UK to hold a 2 Gold Star Great Taste Award for a gluten-free bread. In three years of production, Goodness Grains has won 15 Great Taste Awards, six Blas na hÉireann awards and one Free From (UK) award where Goodness Grains' Gluten-free Apple & Cinnamon Danish Pastry was 'Highly Commended' in the competitive Breakfast category. Goodness Grains' products are available throughout Ireland in all major retailers and foodservice establishments.

The Foods of Athenry

Behind Paul and Siobhan Lawless' multi-award-winning business, The Foods of Athenry, is an enthusiastic farm family, who like many farm  families baked breads, tarts and cakes for their own kitchen table (**www.foodsofathenry.ie**). Siobhan started by asking a local restaurant whether they would take her brown bread. The restaurant took 10 loaves. The following week, the order was for 40 – and a food business was born. The Lawlesses sold their dairy herd in 2004 and the bakery moved into the now-empty milking parlour.

The business has evolved over the years and now they have two separate bakeries: one baking with wheat and spelt and one baking certified gluten-free. The Foods of Athenry now makes a wide range of bakery products catering to many dietary needs, including gluten-free.

The road was not smooth: a fire gutted all the hard work in June 2011. A case of 'man makes plans, God laughs'. But Paul and Siobhan picked themselves up and got to it again.

The hard work and attention to detail has paid off. Since 2007, The Foods of Athenry has been featured in the *Bridgestone Irish Food Guide*, which lists the 'Best in Ireland' of artisan-produced foods. It is a member of Good Food Ireland. And, between 2008 and 2012, it carried off 25 taste awards for a cross-section of products, rubbishing the myth that healthier food is boring or less tasty. The newly-launched gluten-free range is in fun funky packaging, all the colour on the outside!

Cannaboe Confectionery

Sharon Sweeney started making and decorating cakes in her kitchen in Ballinamore, Co. Leitrim, before building a state-of-the-art bakery next to her house. She produces high-quality  celebration cakes, made to order, from the freshest ingredients. Cannaboe (**www.cacamilis.ie**) specialises in and is well-known for wedding cakes but also makes novelty cakes. At one stage, Sharon also produced handmade chocolates. More recently, she has produced two DVDs, which give a step-by-step guide on how to cover and decorate cakes from the comfort of your own home, along with tips and recipes.

One thing that Sharon has always been strong on is updating her skills and over the years she has taken part in many cake, chocolate and skills development courses in Ireland and the UK.

Useful Resources

- Andrews Food Ingredients (**www.andrewsingredients.co.uk**);
- Bakery Bits (**www.bakerybits.co.uk**);
- Easy Equipment: For wicker bread baskets (**www.easyequipment.ie**);
- G&S Services Bakery Equipment Ltd (**www.gandsbakeryequipment.co.uk**);
- McGrath Bakery Services Ltd: New and used equipment (**www.mbs-ltd.org**);
- Scobie Bakery: For when you go big time! (**www.scobiebakery.com**);
- Sugarcraft.ie: A large selection of home-baking and cake-decorating equipment (**www.sugarcraft.ie**);
- The Knead for Bread (**www.thekneadforbread.com**).

11

JAMS, HONEY AND PRESERVES

Introduction

Two of the most popular foods to be made at home for sale locally are bread and jam. In recent years, many home-producers have been foraging in the hedgerows and gardens and started making jam, apple jelly, lemon curd, fruit coulis, quince cheese (a sliceable, jelly-like preserve) and other preserves. All of these are relatively low-risk from a food safety and hygiene point of view, and fairly easy to make in your home kitchen. People love home-made jam and your local shop is a good outlet, especially since many of these products have a long shelf life. So, if you have fruit trees, bushes, or canes, a glut of rhubarb, or access to fresh fruit (whether from your own garden or a local grower or a fruit distributor), then this could be the start you are looking for.

One word of caution though: because it is relatively easy to make these products in your kitchen and because they are relatively low-risk, then the danger is that everyone else will be doing it too, which will mean competition for you. So, do something different – even just slightly different.

Opportunity

There are very many jam producers in the country: some large scale, some small. Don't let this put you off. If you have a good product and have no local competition from other home-based producers, then consumers will be happy to try your jam. What will make them buy it again? The usual suspects: quality, taste and flavour. So, spend time developing your recipe.

If you can come up with a good recipe for strawberry jam, which is notoriously difficult to make as it doesn't set easily (since it contains low levels of pectin), then you could be on to a winner! Jams made with no added sugar (using fruit juice instead usually) are also very popular. The higher the fruit content in your jam, generally the better it will be.

Ingredients and Production Requirements

The basic ingredients required for making jam, jelly or marmalade are fruit, sugar, acid, pectin and water. As with all food products, the fresher the ingredients, the better the product. Use only the best quality fruit, ensure it is just ripe and not bruised or damaged.

The acid and pectin content of fruit is important to consider, as these are required in order to achieve a good 'set' in the jam when the mixture cools down. All fruits contain pectin, but some have higher quantities than others. Apples, gooseberries, blackcurrants and redcurrants are all rich in pectin, whereas strawberries, cherries and pears contain very low levels of pectin. Blackberries, plums and raspberries contain medium amounts of pectin. For fruits with low / medium amounts of pectin, you may need to add commercial pectin to the recipe in order to ensure a good set. This is added when the fruit has been cooked and the flesh and skin have softened.

To test for pectin content, take one teaspoon of the juice from the cooked fruit, place it into a clear glass and allow it to cool for a couple of minutes. Then add three teaspoons of methylated spirits (which you can buy in a pharmacy or DIY shop). If a large firm clot forms, this indicates that the pectin levels are high and there is no need to add extra pectin. If you get a number of broken clumps, this indicates that there is insufficient pectin to get a good set, so a little commercial pectin should be added.

Follow the suppliers' instructions when using a commercial pectin, as often the boiling time will be shorter after sugar has been added. The acidity of the fruit pulp also will influence the set, and as with pectin, fruits also differ in their acidity. Citrus fruits are acidic, while many other fruits such as blackberries, plums and raspberries have medium amounts, and strawberries and cherries are not at all acidic. When making jams with medium / low acid fruit, add one or two tablespoons of fresh lemon juice per kg of fruit at the beginning of cooking.

Commercial jams often contain less than 50g fruit per 100g. Home-based jam-makers should be aiming for 60g fruit/100g jam or higher, ideally. The legal minimum requirement is 35g/100g generally, although blackcurrants and quinces can be 25g/100g and there are some other exceptions. 'Extra jam' contains higher levels of fruit than the usual version. The additional fruit can be added in purée form.

Sometimes you will see labels on jam listing 'jam sugar' as an ingredient. This is sugar with pectin mixed into it (as it's a compound ingredient, the pectin should be listed separately, see **Chapter 7** for ingredients labelling requirements). Jam sugar often contains citric acid also, which acts as a preservative.

The FSAI guide lists the permitted ingredients in jam. Some of these are very specific, depending on the type of jam you are making. For example, red fruit juices can be used only in jam manufactured from rosehips, strawberries, raspberries, gooseberries, redcurrants, plums and rhubarb. Check the guide if you're not sure.

The legislation that tells you all this is EU *Directive 2001/116/EC*, if you fancy a read! The FSAI has a great guide called *Labelling of Jams, Jellies and Marmalade* on its website (**www.fsai.ie**) and the Food Standards Agency (UK and NI) also has a specific Guidance Note in relation to *Jams and Similar Products* (**www.food.gov.uk**).

Teagasc has produced a fact sheet *Small Scale Production of Fruit Preserves*, which you can find on **www.teagasc.ie**.

What You Need
You need:

- Suitable, approved premises;
- A clean pot or vessel for boiling and simmering the fruit – don't use copper or unsealed cast iron pans as the natural acids in fruit will damage the surfaces of these pans, spoiling your jam / preserve;
- A method for sterilising the clean jars;
- An area where you can pour the hot jam into jars;

- A labelling area where the labels are applied to the jars after the lids are on;
- A room to store the packaged product.

Set-up Costs

Set-up costs include the price of the equipment, although your own pots and pans may suffice to begin with.

You will need space – although you might be surprised at first at how few jars you seem to get from a large amount of fruit and sugar and all your hard work!

Running Costs

The main running costs involved are ingredients (fruit, sugar, pectin, fruit juice if you are using it), packaging, electricity and labour. It is important that you include your own time into any cost calculations. Labour input can be high! The cost of marketing and distribution is extra.

You also will have to buy jars, lids, and labels. You must buy new jam jars every time. Legally, you are not allowed to re-use old jars from your cupboard (or anyone else's cupboard!) for your jam enterprise.

Sterilising Jars

There are a number of different ways that you can sterilise jars: oven, microwave or dishwasher. Ask your EHO or Inspector which one they would prefer you to use. The key thing to check, however, is that the jar must be absolutely clean first.

Return on Investment

The price you can sell your jam for will be higher than commercially-produced jam – consumers expect it to be more expensive. Check local shops and see what other home-made jam is being sold for. Around €2.99 or higher is not uncommon – although you need to allow for the retailer's margin too.

How to Make Jam and Preserves

Every jam-maker claims that they have a special skill when it comes to their own recipes, and perhaps they do! It's best to make jam in relatively small quantities to give you better colour, flavour and clarity. The overall method is more or less as follows:

Wash fruit well

Place in a large pot with a little water and some lemon juice (lemon juice is needed to release the natural pectin for some fruits)

Bring to a boil

Add sugar (if you add it too soon to soft fruit with skins such as blueberries, the skin becomes tough and the fruit won't burst)

Stir really well until all the sugar has fully dissolved

Keep boiling until jam reaches 104-106°C, setting temperature (use a jam thermometer)

Remove from the heat and take off any scum (especially for marmalade)

Pour into clean sterilised jars straight away

Put on lids immediately

Allow to cool before labelling

To test jam to see whether it is cooked enough and will set, you can:

- Dip a wooden spoon into the jam, holding the bowl of the spoon facing you. If the jam is ready, then two or three large drops will roll along the edge of the spoon forming almost a triangle of thick jam;
- Drop a teaspoon of jam onto a chilled saucer (chill the saucer in the freezer or fridge first); the jam should cool quickly to room temperature and thicken up;
- Put a spoonful of jam onto a plate, push the jam with your finger and if the skin wrinkles, then the jam is ready.

Otherwise, boil it up again.

Current Trends and Future Developments

Quince cheese, port-flavoured cranberry sauce, mixed fruit jams, jellies and various savoury chutneys are increasingly popular. Consumers expect a choice, so if you want to differentiate yourself from the herd, then produce high-quality, good-flavour, seasonal varieties.

Specific Labelling Issues

Jam, Extra Jam, Jelly, Extra Jelly and Marmalade
The usual labelling information is mandatory, as already described in **Chapter 7**. In particular, note the following:

- **The name under which the product is sold:** For example, 'Raspberry Jam';
- **Instructions for use, where necessary:** For example, 'Reduced sugar jams must be kept in the fridge'.

The following labelling information is also mandatory under the specific labelling rules:

- **An indication of the fruit used in descending order:** For example, for rhubarb and ginger jam;
- **The fruit content:** By including the words 'prepared with Xg of fruit per 100g';

- **The total sugar content:** By the words 'total sugar content Xg per 100g'.

Where the residual content of sulphur dioxide exceeds 10mg/ kg, you must indicate its presence on the list of ingredients – though most home-producers won't need to worry about this at all.

Very important! The name of the product, the fruit content and the total sugar content must appear in the same visual fields and in clearly visible characters.

Honey

You will be forgiven if you don't remember the great honey scandal of 2006! It was found that, of a number of producers surveyed, some were mislabelling their honey, claiming it was Irish when it was not. Local honey is always popular among shoppers, though the recent poor summers have reduced the volume of honey available. So, if you do produce Irish honey, then shout about it! There is a very useful factsheet on *Honey Production* on **www.teagasc.ie**.

If you keep bees and produce honey for sale, then you must register as a 'primary producer'. You can get the form from your local DAFM office or download it from **www.agriculture.gov.ie** (search for "Registration as a Primary Producer of Honey") or contact the Food Standards Agency (**www.food.gov.uk**).

There are very specific rules relating to the labelling of honey. Products can only be marketed as 'honey' if they comply with the definition and compositional requirements as set out in *Directive 2001/110/EC* relating to honey.

Some of the most common types of honey are as follows:

- **According to origin:** Such as blossom honey or nectar honey (honey obtained from the nectar of plants);
- **According to mode of production and / or presentation:** Such as chunk honey or cut comb in honey (honey that contains one or more pieces of comb honey).

The country or countries of origin where the honey has been harvested must be indicated on the label. If the honey originates in more than one

EU Member State or third country, then the indication may be replaced by one of the following as appropriate:

- 'blend of EC honeys';
- 'blend of non-EC honeys'; or
- 'blend of EC and non-EC honeys'.

Case Studies

Mileeven Fine Foods

Mileeven (**www.mileeven.com**) was established in 1988 in Kilkenny by Eilis Gough from her hobby of beekeeping. Two good summers back to back gave a surplus of honey, which lead Eilis to do research on the honey market in Ireland and, from those results, Mileeven was established. The name comes from the Irish words "Mil" for honey and "aoibhinn" for delightful and, true to its name, that's still what Mileeven produces today.

Eilis has gone on to expand the range over the years to meet the demand for differentiation and because there is always a limited supply of Irish honey due to the Irish weather. *Sarah's Honey* is one range of newer honeys that has delicious additions – nuts, fruits or spices such as ginger or mango – that change the flavour.

Mileeven now supplies all the major retailers in Ireland, as well as exporting to over 15 countries, dealing with top stores around the world like UK-based Sainsbury's and Harrods and Dean & Deluca in the Middle East.

Mileeven's success is down to hard work and a dedicated team, as well as always being open to innovation and differentiation in response to market demand.

Westport Grove Jams and Chutneys

After a lifetime working in the pharmaceutical and health care industries, Sean Casey started making jam at home in his kitchen in 2008, purely as a hobby at first. He saw a gap in the local market and

decided to focus on jams. When I first met
Sean a couple of years ago, he told me that if
there was nothing on television, he would
wander out to the kitchen and cook up a
batch of jam. If anyone was looking for him,
his family would know where to find him!

Sean saw a gap in the local market and
approached local shops to see whether there was an interest; he asked
them what cost they expected the product to be delivered to them for;
he already knew their selling price; he looked for suppliers and
determined his costs for each product as he needed to know what his
margin would be; and he sent samples to an approved micro lab to
validate his shelf life (Best Before dates).

In December 2011, his business moved into a new, dedicated facility
built behind the house. Sean now also makes sugar-free jams, chocolate
spread, nougat, quince cheese and chocolate orange slices. He has also
upgraded his labels and jars to focus on the luxury end of the market.

Erin Grove Preserves

Jayne Paget grew up on the
family farm just outside
Enniskillen in Co. Fermanagh,
in Northern Ireland, where

her grandmother grew a wide range of fruit and vegetables. Jayne
spent summer days picking strawberries, raspberries, blackcurrants,
gooseberries and rhubarb in the garden and learned how to make jam.
The surplus jam was sold through Jayne's aunt's home bakery in
Enniskillen, giving her both a source of income, and also the realisation
that there was a ready market for good quality home-made products.

Jayne qualified and worked as a Home Economics teacher for
several years, and then in 2001, funding from the Women in
Agriculture farm diversification programme gave Jayne the start she
needed and Erin Grove was born!

Jayne wanted to maintain the ethos of producing a top quality
product using the best quality ingredients to produce a range of

products that are bursting with colour and flavour and that would give Erin Grove (**www.eringrove.com**) a point of difference from the mass-produced brands. Everything is made by hand in small batches, using the original recipes, in the same way her grandmother made them on the kitchen stove. Along the way, a range of chutneys was added and Erin Grove now has almost 40 different products, which have won 10 Great Taste Awards.

Useful Resources

- County Dublin Beekeepers' Association (**www.dublinbees.org**);
- Federation of Irish Beekeepers' Associations (**www.irishbeekeeping.ie**);
- Grow It Yourself (GIY) (**www.giyinternational.org**);
- Quickcrop (**www.quickcrop.ie**).

12

DUCK EGGS

Introduction

Duck eggs fell out of fashion in the latter part of the 20th century, demand fell rapidly and commercial egg producers ignored ducks in favour of the more easily farmed chicken. While duck eggs are not very widely available still, they can be found in some supermarkets, farm shops, and farmers' markets – and there is considerable anecdotal evidence of unregistered eggs being sold (illegally!) under the counter, as it were. It is really important to know that, while there is no specific legislation that requires duck eggs to be stamped, if you plan to use them then you should make sure that your supplier is registered as a food business operator and that the eggs are properly labelled, at the very least. Duck eggs are generally all either free range or organic.

A duck egg can be used as a direct substitute for a normal hen's egg. The yolks are larger and higher in fat than a hen's egg, which makes them richer with their own distinctive flavour. In baking, duck eggs work really well, so many home bakers use them in preference to hen eggs.

There also has been an increase in the popularity of duck eggs for eating. As a result, there is an opportunity for new and existing duck egg producers to meet this market demand.

History

In 2010, there was a major outbreak of *Salmonellosis* in Ireland, which was associated with the consumption of undercooked duck eggs or consumption of raw foods made with duck eggs. The problem was that, up until this time, there were few, if any, controls in place for duck egg production and control.

However, subsequently, control measures have been implemented in order to attempt to restore consumer confidence.

While most sales to date have been from small-scale producers selling at farmers' markets or from the farm gate, on-going improvements in production and control standards will help to generate customer trust and so bring duck eggs back into popularity.

Duck Egg *vs* Hen Egg

A health benefit claimed for duck eggs is that some people who have an allergic reaction to hen eggs are able to eat duck eggs without any adverse reaction, though I've only got anecdotal evidence for this, no hard scientific fact.

Duck eggs have more albumen (protein in the egg white) than a chicken egg. Fans of duck eggs say that scrambled eggs and omelettes made with them are richer in flavour. Duck eggs are especially useful in baking, given the higher proportion of yolk to white – bakers report that the additional protein gives cakes and buns more 'lift'.

While duck eggs can be used in the same way as hen eggs when baking or cooking, you will need to do some calculations to take the difference in size and weight into account. The average weight of a duck egg is approximately 80 grams, while an average hen egg is about 50 grams. Care should be taken not to overcook duck eggs, as their higher water content tends to make them rubbery. The shells of duck eggs are thicker than hen eggs, which, generally gives them a longer shelf life.

Best Breeds for Duck Egg Production

The breed most commonly used for egg production is the Khaki Campbell, a medium-sized brown duck that should have a flock life of three to four years. It produces on average 300 eggs per year, provided that proper management and feeding are carried out. Khaki Campbells are very active with a sturdy and upright posture. They are extremely hardy and are at home on land as well as water.

The Pekin breed of duck will lay between 150 and 180 eggs per year.

The Chiltern Duck is a hybrid duck, often confused with the Aylesbury apparently. Chilterns are specially bred for laying, laying 350 slightly off-white-tinted eggs per year that are larger on average than Khaki Campbells. The ducklings are very fast growers, easily reared and hardy.

The Aylesbury duck is primarily a meat duck, producing excellent meat and in excess of 100 eggs per year. The Aylesbury duck is an old duck and, in some parts, a rare breed but it used to be one of the main meat-producing ducks kept by smallholders in large quantities up until WWII. It is still a very good duck for the smallholder and home producer to keep. It will reach up to 10lb in weight at around nine weeks but in order to reach this, the ducks must be fed a high-quality grain diet.

Khaki Campbell

Pekin

Indian Runner

Another good egg producer is the Indian Runner, which can produce over 250 eggs per year.

You might expect the following output volumes (eggs/year):

	Total *pa* / bird	Packs / bird @ 6 / box
Aylesbury	100	16
Chiltern	350	58
Indian Runner	250	41
Khaki Campbell	300	50
Pekin	180	30

General Requirements

Guidelines for Producers of Small Quantities of Duck Eggs (Backyard Flocks) is available from the DAFM website (**www.agriculture.gov.ie**).

Ducks are social animals and need the company of other ducks; they do not keep very well as solitary birds. Ducks need a dry solid duck house / coop for sleep and shelter, as well as fresh clean grass. They are at risk of predators so a predator-proof enclosure would be useful, though not everyone is able to provide one, and many duck farmers prefer their birds to roam free in the fields. Unlike hens, ducks must have a pond or pool of fresh, clean, water in which they can refresh themselves. The water must deep enough for them to submerge their whole head, which they need to do in order to keep their eyes moist.

As with all poultry, you should control the entry of unauthorised personnel or vehicles that might bring in infection. Salmonella can spread from ducks to other poultry species, animals and humans. The perimeter of the site should be clearly identified and, if possible, fenced.

Ducks can be very messy as their droppings are wet, so regular cleaning of their housing is important. Also, if they are confined to a small patch of ground, it is very important that the birds are moved regularly to fresh ground, otherwise problems will occur.

Duck Houses

Duck housing does not differ significantly from other poultry housing, except that ducks do not need perches. Artificial lighting should be provided if you want all-year-round production (16 hours of light per day). Houses consist of a slatted area and a veranda or litter area. There must be dry litter on the floor of the building to absorb the droppings, and this will need to be changed regularly to reduce any chance of disease.

Ducks need good size egg-laying nests of at least 12" (300mm) square or preferably larger. These also need to be of sufficient depth – around 8" (200mm) lined with deep straw, which again will need to be changed regularly because ducks can come in wet from the outside.

The building can be made from anything as long as it is dry and it can be much lower in height than other poultry houses as ducks are ground-dwellers. In good weather, the ducks may not use the housing at all except to lay.

Clean, fresh drinking water must be available 24 hours a day and the drinking vessel must be deep enough for the ducks to submerge all of their beaks. Fresh drinking water should be changed at least twice daily.

Feeding Ducks

Ducks will eat almost anything and will consume a lot of grass and vegetation – even insects. In fact, some are prolific slug-eaters, so they become the gardener's friend. As they have access to clean, free-ranging, fresh vegetation, farmers could make their own feed from crushed or rolled grain. Chicks require special chick crumb for the first six to eight weeks of their lives.

Code of Practice

The *Code of Practice for Duck Table Egg Producers (2010)*, issued by DAFM, is available on **www.agriculture.gov.ie**, and includes the general requirements for the rearing of point-of-lay ducks for the production of table eggs and the general requirements for egg production systems.

The Code of Practice covers sourcing of flocks from a registered operator, implementing a Salmonella monitoring programme and stamping of eggs with a producer code to provide traceability. For more information, including legislation controlling duck eggs, duck egg producers should seek advice from recognised sources and consult the relevant and current guidelines / publications produced by DAFM and other bodies.

Legislation and Food Safety

Registration

All flocks, including backyard flocks, must be registered with DAFM. You will find application forms available for download on the Department's website.

The purpose of registration, which is a relatively easy process, is simply to ensure that DAFM has a full picture of where poultry are located, so that it can alert owners quickly in the event of a disease outbreak and also give advice on appropriate precautionary, containment and control measures as soon as possible.

Food Safety

Some advice for the safe usage of duck eggs:

- Duck eggs should not be eaten raw;
- Only eat duck eggs that have been thoroughly cooked, until both the white and yolk are solid;
- If you are preparing a dish that contains duck eggs, ensure that you have cooked it thoroughly before eating it;
- Do not use raw duck eggs in the preparation of products that contain raw or lightly cooked egg, such as homemade mayonnaise, tiramisu, icing or hollandaise sauce;
- When using duck eggs in cooking or baking, do not eat or taste the raw mix;
- After handling raw duck eggs, always wash your hands thoroughly;
- Ensure all utensils and preparation surfaces that have been in contact with raw duck eggs are washed thoroughly before being re-used;
- Store duck eggs in the fridge away from ready-to-eat foods.

Bord Bia Egg Quality Assurance Scheme

The Egg Quality Assurance Scheme (EQAS) in place for hen eggs does not currently apply to duck eggs; therefore, duck eggs cannot carry the quality assurance logo. Duck eggs are not included in the egg marketing regulations either and therefore they do not have to carry markings on the egg itself to indicate the Best Before date or traceability information. However, this information should be included on the packaging, or on the accompanying documentation if there is no packaging.

While duck eggs are not covered by the EQAS, it is recommended that producers should work towards these requirements, as any revision of the standard in future may include duck eggs.

Labelling

While hen eggs marketed in the EU must be graded by quality and weight and be packed, labelled, stored, transported and presented for sale in accordance with legislation on the marketing standards for eggs, no similar scheme is currently in place for duck eggs. However, duck egg producers are encouraged to comply with the general requirements as best practice.

It is recommended that boxes / packs of duck eggs should be labelled similarly to hen eggs. Eggs sold in boxes / packs therefore should have the following displayed on the packaging:

- **Name, address and identification number (approval number) of the packing centre:** You will get this once you register with DAFM;
- **Best Before date:** Use an ink stamp that you can apply by hand;
- Number of eggs in the pack;
- Advice to consumers to keep eggs refrigerated after purchase.

Where eggs are not sold in packs, retailers are required to display labelling information with each batch of eggs. As noted above, this labelling must be clearly visible to the customer and should include:

- Identification number (approval number) of the packing centre;
- Best Before date;

- Advice to consumers to keep eggs refrigerated after purchase;
- An indication of farming method used.

Note: A batch is defined as "eggs from the same source with the same Best Before date and the same quality and weight grading".

If you are not sure what labelling information to put on the eggs or boxes, just ask your local inspector who you will get to know once you register with them.

Distribution and Marketing

Eggs are highly perishable, with a short shelf life. So, it is absolutely essential that you identify your market and customers before committing to setting up a duck egg venture. While this may not be as important for other areas of new business development, it is absolutely essential for perishable poultry and eggs.

The production and marketing of duck eggs is financially viable only when you can charge more for them than readily-available/ mass-produced hen eggs.

Who Is My Market?

Bakers consider duck eggs to function better than hen eggs, and home bakers in particular often favour them. Demand for duck eggs is strong in Chinese and Asian communities, where salted duck eggs and other delicacies are popular, and so producers should consider addressing this particular ethnic market.

The Economics of Production

Buildings or conversions for providing duck houses will be the greatest part of the investment cost.

For small-scale production, supplying farm-gate sales or farmers' markets, the upgrading of an existing bird-house is the most cost-effective option. Equipment needed for the flock includes feeders, drinkers, nest boxes and slats. A feed store is needed, as is fencing. Automatic drinkers are essential regardless of flock size, while other equipment choice will be governed by flock size.

Requirement for investment capital depends on where you are starting from, how many ducks you plan to have and whether everything will be done by hand or if you plan to have some automation. Teagasc advises that assessment of needs and costs is typically carried out on a case-by-case basis, and so calculating costs is not standard.

As a guide, birds may cost between €3 and €9 each. Websites such as Done Deal (**www.donedeal.ie**) and Gumtree (**www.gumtree.co.uk**) list many suppliers, but it is essential that birds and eggs are purchased only from a registered, reliable source. Registration fees are in the region of €100. Other costs include testing fees for water and faecal samples.

Eggs typically sell for between €2.20 and €3.99 for six, depending on the shop. The shop will take its margin, so unless you are selling direct to consumer then remember the retail price is not the price you will get. So, your income, based on 100 birds, might be:

Breed	Number of Packs @ 6 eggs / box	Sell to shop for €2 / box €	Gross Annual income (100 birds)* €
Aylesbury	16	32	3,200
Chiltern	58	116	11,600
Indian Runner	41	82	8,200
Khaki Campbell	50	100	10,000
Pekin	30	60	6,000

This calculation does not take into account the costs of housing, feed, testing, transport, packaging, etc.

Value-added

The potential for adding value to duck eggs is limited. However, salted duck eggs are popular on the Asian market. Demand for duck eggs may be led by the Chinese and Asian communities, and so producers should consider looking at these markets.

The practice of salting duck eggs may have started as a method of preservation, but salted duck eggs are now considered a delicacy. Salting makes the egg whites dense and almost rubbery in appearance, but it is the yolk that is especially prized. If properly salted, the duck egg yolks are creamy, granular, and oily all at once – an unusual texture that tastes especially rich and salty.

Salted duck eggs are available ready-salted, cooked, and vacuum-packed at many Chinese or specialist grocery stores.

Future Developments

The regularisation of duck egg production will continue to benefit all reputable producers, as some backyard producers had brought duck eggs into disrepute in recent years. Duck egg producers require support as changing from old methods to new documentation and procedures will pose a challenge to many.

Case Studies

Quinn's Quacks

Bernie Quinn has 120 free-range ducks on her farm outside Ballyhaunis, Co. Mayo, where she has been operating since 1991. She is a registered and approved producer and currently supplies several shops and supermarkets across the region.

Parkview Farm

Parkview Farm is a family-run business in Tourlestrane, South Sligo, producing free range duck eggs (**www.parkviewduckfarm.com**). The business was established in 2009 by the Mulgrew family, who personally tend their flock of over 800 ducks. The

ducks are bedded on fresh clean straw at night-time.

Glenfin Farm

Brian Phelan is the owner-manager of Glenfin Farm (**www.glenfinfarm.ie**), a business based in Co. Monaghan that has become a leading distributor of award-winning duck eggs in Ireland. Brian set up the business in 2008, and now has a total of 2,500 ducks, with

each one producing an egg a day. With two vans, he works with distributors to supply his eggs to specialist food stores and butcher shops around the country.

Useful Resources

- DAFM, Pigmeat and Poultry Section:
  - o **www.agriculture.gov.iefarmingsectors/poultry** has information/forms available to download;
  - o Local advisors and offices are located all around the country;
- Teagasc has a poultry advisor (**www.teagasc.ie**);
- Bord Bia (**www.bordbia.ie**);
- *Guidelines for Producers of Small Quantities of Duck Eggs* – available from the Food Safety Authority of Ireland (**www.fsai.ie**);
- Irish Farmers Association (**www.ifa.ie**):
  - o Alo Mohan, Chairman of National Poultry Committee, (087) 629 2456;

- o Amii Cahill, Executive Secretary of National Poultry Committee, (01) 450 0266;
- **Useful websites:**
  - o Irish Fowl: Includes a Directory of Irish poultry breeders (though not exhaustive) (**www.irishfowl.com**);
  - o Irish-Poultry.com: Includes list of upcoming poultry sales and shows in Ireland (**www.irish-poultry.com**);
  - o Poultry Ireland: Good general resource with links to other sites, events listing (**www.poultry.ie**);
  - o *Practical Poultry* magazine (**www.practicalpoultry.co.uk**);
  - o Rainbow Free Range Poultry (**www.freerangepoultry.ie**);
- **Suppliers:**
  - o Billy Bob's Pet & Country Superstore: Poultry equipment and housing (**www.billybobs.ie**);
  - o Connacht Gold: Full range of agri-supplies (**www.connachtgold.ie**);
  - o Farm supply stores and co-ops listed in *Golden Pages* or local newspapers;
  - o Local poultry clubs: Great for support and information;
  - o MacEoin Poultry Supplies Ltd (**www.maceoinltd.com**);
  - o Old McDonald's Farm & Feed Store: Egg boxes and stamping kits (**www.oldmcdonald.ie**);
  - o Straw Chip: housing and bedding.

13

ICE CREAM, YOGURT, CHEESE AND BUTTER

Introduction

For a long time, the only yogurt or ice cream you could buy was that made by very large companies; although a variety of cheeses was available, there were only a few butter producers. All that has changed, even in the last five years. So, here we look at how you might go about developing a range of dairy products – for example, farmhouse or home-made cheese, ice cream, yogurt, butter or even kefir (a fermented drink).

As with all new foods, the main force driving the market for dairy products comes from consumer trends. Now that the milk quota is gone, non-farmers can purchase milk from farmers without restriction. However, getting the milk is the easy part, as the barriers to entry for dairy products are high in terms of costs and legislation. Registration and approval of premises making dairy produce falls under DAFM's remit in the Republic of Ireland.

Cheese

Farmhouse cheese-making virtually died out in Ireland until the late 1970s. For at least 25 years before then, cheese-making in Ireland had been confined almost exclusively to large-scale factory production, mainly concentrating on cheddar production and mainly owned by the big dairy co-ops. However, today Ireland produces more cheese varieties *per capita* than any other country in the world, according to the

National Dairy Council. The production of quality Irish cheese has expanded to the extent that there are over 30 members of Cáis, the Association of Irish Farmhouse Cheese-makers (**www.irishcheese.ie**), including makers of cow, goat, sheep and even buffalo cheese.

The story about the cheese – its provenance – is of particular importance when branding and marketing cheese. Irish cheeses are associated not only with where they are made but also often with the individual cheese-makers themselves. Traceability of Irish farmhouse cheese can extend not just to a region or townland, but also often to a family.

The Opportunity

As you might expect, the majority of cheese producers in Ireland were traditionally located in the major dairy-producing counties in the south of the country. Now, there are several artisan cheese producers in Ireland north of the Galway-Dublin line, such as Andrew Pelham Burn of Carrowholly in Westport and Marion Roeleweld of Killeen Farmhouse Cheese (**www.killeencheese.ie**) in Galway. Silke Croppe of Corleggy Cheeses (**www.corleggycheeses.com**) in Cavan makes cheese with raw milk. In Northern Ireland, you'll find City Cheese (**www.citycheese.co.uk**), made from organic raw milk, and Dart Mountain Cheese (**www.dartmountaincheese.com**) in the Sperrin Mountains, Co. Derry, as well as bigger producers like Farmview Dairies (**www.farmviewdairies.net**) and Fivemiletown Creamery's (**www.fivemiletowncheese.com**) cheese range (owned by Dale Farm). Back down South, you can get Buffalo Mozzarella cheese in Co. Cork (**macroombuffalocheese.com**) and Bluebell Falls Goats' Cheese in Co. Clare (**www.bluebellfalls.com**).

Market and Distribution

The main market for farmhouse cheese is the island of Ireland, although some producers are exporting. As with any new food, it is essential to carry out market research in advance to determine what gaps there may be in the market, whether local or national.

Almost all supermarkets now have artisan cheeses in their main fridges, as do many smaller and specialist shops. Horgan's in Mitchelstown (**www.horgans.com**) is one of the largest countrywide distributors of specialist cheese. The Traditional Cheese Company (**www.traditionalcheese.ie**) supplies retail and wholesale brands nationwide, the majority of which are produced in Ireland. Many small producers are reaching the shelves through the SuperValu / Bord Bia Food Academy programme. The Bord Bia *Guide to Farmhouse Cheese*, available on **www.bordbia.ie**, also identifies opportunities for farmhouse cheese on the home and export markets.

Production

There is a useful *Farmhouse Cheese Factsheet* available on **www.teagasc.ie**, which gives some facts and figures and describes the general production methods. Note that quark and soft cheeses are considerably easier to make compared to hard cheese varieties.

According to Eddie O'Neill, author of the Teagasc *Factsheet*, what you need are:

- Suitable approved premises;
- A stainless steel vessel where milk can be converted into cheese;
- A moulding / pressing area where the curds are formed into their final shape;
- A brine tank (most cheeses) to salt the cheese;
- A ripening room where the cheese is held under the right conditions of temperature and humidity;
- A packaging area where the cheese is weighed and packed prior to distribution;
- A cold room or refrigerator to store the packaged product.

The FSAI and Teagasc have a workbook called *HACCP / Food Safety Workbook for Farmhouse Cheesemakers*, which is available on request.

Set-up Costs

Set-up costs include the price of the equipment, premises and/or conversion of existing buildings. You may have an existing building on your property, such as your garage or an old barn or outhouse, that could be converted into cheese-making units. It is extremely difficult to give indicative figures for costs where the conversion of existing buildings is required, as the work required will vary from one premises to another, depending on its state of repair. Whether a new premises or conversion, the costs of ensuring that the buildings meet hygiene regulations could be high. Advice on conversion requirements can be given on an individual basis by your DAFM advisor or Inspector.

The range of equipment needed can cost anything between €10,000 and €30,000. Some equipment suppliers are listed at the end of this chapter.

Running Costs

The main direct costs involved are milk, ingredients, electricity, packaging and labour. It takes about 10 litres of milk to make 1kg of cheddar cheese. Rennet costs typically €3 to €4 per 50ml. It is important that producers cost their own time into any business plan/ cost calculations, as the labour input can be high.

The cost of marketing and distribution is extra, and distribution costs in particular can affect the overall viability of the business.

How Is Cheese Made?

Every cheese-maker has their own little secrets about their recipe and what they do at each step to distinguish their cheese from the others. Take a look at *The Craft of Cheese-making* on **www.bordbia.ie**. There are over 500 varieties of cheese recognised by the International Dairy Federation and over 1,000 in a 2011 study. The more moisture there is in the cheese, the softer it will be.

Some cheese must be kept to mature for a time, at a particular temperature and with certain other conditions to produce the quality and flavour desired. Some examples include Cheddar, Gruyère and Parmigiano Reggiano.

Here is a general overview of cheese-making:

Pour milk into a vat or container

Add starter culture to ripen the milk

Add rennet to produce curds and whey

Separate the curds from the whey

Press the curds into moulds

Turn the moulds to form the shape and release more whey

Apply pressure if a hard cheese is being made

Add salt, if required

Leave it to ripen (if desired)

Pack and label

Off to the shops!

Return on Investment

The price you can sell your cheese for will vary depending on whether it is a speciality cheese and how far you are away from your market (as distribution costs will impact on your price). The period from production to time of sale could be up to six months, so being realistic, it is highly likely that cheese producers will have a negative cash flow in their first year.

Current Trends and Future Developments

Irish specialist cheeses have an international reputation for flavour and quality. Goat's cheese is now commonplace.

There are a few cheese-makers who use raw milk in the production of their cheeses. Caution is key when it comes to working with raw milk, and it is best to follow advice. A very high level of hygiene management is critical to ensure food safety when using raw milk, as raw milk may contain disease-causing bacteria if not handled properly. The FSAI has issued a leaflet to this effect: *Health Risks from Unpasteurised Milk, 2009*, which is available to download on **www.fsai.ie**. The regulations on using and selling raw milk and raw milk products vary between Scotland, Northern Ireland, England and Wales. Check out **www.food.gov.uk** for information.

For information on members of Cáis, the Association of Irish Farmhouse Cheese-makers, see the website **www.irishcheese.ie**.

Case Study – Cheese

Carrowholly Cheese

Carrowholly Cheese is a multi-award-winning Gouda-style farmhouse cheese made on the shores of Clew Bay on Ireland's scenic Atlantic coastline. It is made from raw cow's milk, collected from local farmers. Each cheese is made by hand by Andrew Pelham Burn (**carrowhollycheese@gmail.com**) and

production is kept intentionally small so as to ensure the outstanding quality of this cheese. Andrew sometimes runs cheese-making courses, so if you're interested, contact him for details!

Dozio's of Mayo

A newcomer is Dozio's of Mayo, making Swiss Zincarlin and Furmagella cow's milk cheese near Charlestown. Danilo, who is originally from Switzerland, and

Helen make two types of cheese using the ancient recipes from Canton Ticino in the south of Switzerland from locally sourced milk in Helen's homeplace in County Mayo. The Furmagella and Zincarlin recipes were adapted and the 'Ella', a semi-hard cheese with a mild, buttery taste, and

'Zing', a soft cheese, hand-rolled into logs and available in Natural, Black Pepper & Garlic, Sun-dried Tomatoes and Ginger & Chili flavours were launched in 2016.

Smoked Cheese – Knockanore

Eamonn Lonergan has been making Knockanore Farmhouse Cheese for 30 years using full cream, raw cows' milk using traditional cheddaring techniques from his pedigree Friesian herd. The cheese is available in vintage red and white, both of which are aged for at least eight months, as  well as varieties with herbs and spices. Knockanore (**www.knockanorecheese.com**) is one of the very few cheeses left in Ireland that can truly be labelled a 'farmhouse' cheese in the true sense, in that it is produced on the farm and using only milk from the farm. It is also one of only a handful of raw milk cheeses still being produced in Ireland.

The most iconic cheese in the range is perhaps the smoked version, which is smoked on the farm using oak sourced locally. This smoked cheese is available as a delicious full wheel or in pre-packed wedges.

Farmhouse or Home-made Ice Cream

Ice cream is made by freezing and aerating a mixture of ingredients, including milk, sugar, flavours and water. The composition of ice cream varies, but is usually about 12% milk fat, 11% non-fat milk solids, 15% sugar and the rest of the ingredients plus water accounting for the balance. The 1952 legislation says that ice cream must have a minimum of 10% sugar, but watch this space, that law is currently under review.

For farmhouse, traditional or home-made ice cream producers, provenance again plays an important role in marketing the product, with the name of the farm, locality or producer often the main focus of the brand.

History

It seems that everyone from the Chinese to the Italians and Americans lay claim to having invented ice cream!

In China, during the Tang period (AD 618-907), buffalo, cows' and goats' milk was heated and allowed to ferment. This 'yogurt' was then mixed with flour for thickening and camphor for flavour and was chilled before being served.

Italian *gelato* dates back to the 16th century. Most stories give the credit to Bernardo Buontalenti, a native of Florence, Italy, who delighted the court of Catherina de Medici with his creation. Italians almost certainly introduced gelato to the rest of Europe, with Sicilian-born Francesco Procopio dei Coltelli being one of the most influential individuals in the history of gelato – he was one of the first to sell it to the public.

In 1843, an American housewife Nancy Johnson invented the hand-cranked ice cream churn. She patented her invention and sold the patent for $200 to a Philadelphia kitchen wholesaler which, by 1847, had made enough freezers to satisfy the high demand. From 1847 to 1877, more than 70 improvements to ice cream churns were patented.

The Market

The market for speciality ice creams has definitely grown in recent years and there are several artisan and farmhouse producers around. The premium or luxury end of the market has grown too and it looks like this trend is set to continue. While consumers are increasingly concerned for their health, indulgence in premium ice cream is growing.

There are several artisan producers all over the island of Ireland, such as Tipperary Organic (**www.tipperaryorganic.ie**) or Baldwin's (**www.baldwinsicecream.com**), Linnalla Farmhouse Icecream (**www.linnallaicecream.ie**) and Fabio's Italian Ice Cream in Sligo. In Northern Ireland, Glastry Farm (**www.glastryfarm.com**) and Morelli's (**www.morellisices.com**) are well-known and there is a lovely wee farmhouse ice cream parlour in Irvinestown, Co. Fermanagh, called Tickety-Moo.

Opportunity

Ireland has the third highest consumption of ice cream *per capita* in Europe, with a retail market value of over €75.8m. In the UK, the market is worth £1bn! The ice cream sector was badly affected by the recession, as have many other luxury or 'special treat' foods. But, if staying in is the new going out, then good quality ice cream will always be in demand as an indulgence. Chocolate flavour is still the top seller.

Consumers usually assume luxury ice cream will be full of dairy cream, so it could be very worthwhile trying to develop reduced fat versions in your range.

Interesting new flavours are a good way to get the consumer's attention – for example, Cinnamon & Cashew, Black Tea, Lemon Curd or Sweet Potato even! Gin & Tonic flavour is another one that caught my attention recently!

For Irish ice cream-makers, there are also opportunities to target consumers who want flavours targeted at children.

Note that you cannot make ice cream allergen-free unless you remove the milk, and then it's not ice cream any longer.

Production Method

You can buy ice cream machines ranging from 1 litre in size up to commercial scale, depending on how big a batch you want to make. You can start making it by hand and then move on to at least a partial batch manufacturing process. The recipe is a matter of trial and error. To use fresh fruit or liquid flavours? To add egg or not? And you will have to play around with the best method to give you the flavour and consistency you want.

Teagasc's *Ice Cream Factsheet* (**www.teagasc.ie**) gives some facts and figures and describes the general commercial production method.

As for all food products, you will need premises that meet the EU hygiene legislation, and you must notify your local EHO or Inspector. For ice cream production, you need an approved processing area, a cold room and a freezer room, an area to store dry ingredients and an area to store packaging. Equipment for processing ranges in price enormously and can be quite expensive.

One method I've come across lately is making ice cream using liquid nitrogen. A little gimmicky perhaps, and a bit dangerous maybe, but it's certainly impressive. If you get a chance, visit Chin Chin Labs in the Camden Market, London to try it yourself (**www.chinchinlabs.com**).

Case Study – Ice Cream

Murphy's Ice Cream

Sean and Kieran Murphy started Murphy's Ice Cream (**www.murphysicecream.ie**) in Dingle, Co. Kerry in 2000, with the goal of making the best ice cream in the world. Murphy's Ice Cream uses milk from the rare, indigenous breed of Kerry cow because the milk is so wonderful (note the provenance!).

Quality and originality are of primary importance – the brothers say that they never use preservatives, colours, mixes, powdered milk, bottled flavours, or anything not natural. They use Dingle seawater to boil down to make sea salt ice cream and fresh mint leaves for the fresh mint ice cream.

Having originally made the ice cream in the back of their shop in Dingle, they soon expanded into bigger production premises and now have six shops across the country as well as selling through other retailers. As they say themselves, "We now have bigger pots and pans, but we still make ice cream the same way – breaking eggs and using fresh cream, milk and pure cane sugar to make a delicious custard that we flavour with fresh, natural, real ingredients".

Some other Irish ice cream producers include:

- Braemar Farm Icecream in Co. Antrim;
- Featherbed Farm Luxury Ice Cream (**www.featherbedfarm.ie**);
- Gino's Gelato, Dublin (**www.ginosgelato.com**);
- Glastry Farm Ice Cream, Co. Down (**www.glastryfarm.com**);
- Happy Days Icecream, Cork (**www.happydaysicecream.ie**);

- Linnalla Ice Cream, Co. Clare (**www.linnallaicecream.ie**);
- Paganini Ice Cream, Wexford (**www.paganini.ie**);
- Rossmore Farmhouse Ice Cream, Co. Laois
  (**www.rossmorefarm.ie**);
- Silver Pail Dairy, Co. Cork (**www.silverpail.com**);
- Valentia Island Farmhouse Dairy, Co. Kerry
  (**www.valentiadairy.com**).

Farmhouse Yogurt and Kefir

Yogurt has been a vital form of calcium in the diet in South Eastern Europe and Asia Minor for thousands of years. However, it was largely unknown outside these regions until scientific research suggested a direct link between yogurt and fermented milk and the unusually long lifespan enjoyed by Bulgarian people. Though this link was never proven, yogurt quickly gained popularity across Europe and the USA, particularly after fruit and sugar was added to improve the flavour and it began to be produced commercially.

Yogurt was introduced into the UK market in the 1960s and was seen as a health food, brought in from Switzerland. It came into the Irish dairy market in the 1970s and soon became a household essential, particularly popular with younger consumers.

The Market

Adults eat the most yogurt, accounting for about 75% of the total market. Family yogurts, especially those aimed at young families, followed by large pots, are most popular. Yogurt is eaten most often for breakfast and as a snack. Diet or low fat yogurts are beginning to lose popularity a bit as consumers become more aware of the ingredients they contain, especially sugar. Indulgence is always attractive for consumers, so yogurts in glass containers or with specialised ingredients like Madagascan Vanilla or with authentic provenance will appeal. The health market continues to grow and yogurts with high protein have emerged. Other trends include sheep's milk yogurt and fermented drinks such as kefir, both targeting the health market.

Opportunity

While there are very many large commercial producers in the market, consumers are always interested in something new and locally-made, and are prepared to pay for it. Shoppers see yogurt as an everyday standard purchase but competition is fierce, it's a very crowded shelf. Any new producer should consider their target market, branding and USPs, particularly if they aim to compete with the big manufacturers.

Production Method (Small Batch)

Yogurt is produced by the bacterial fermentation of milk. The bacteria used to make yogurt are called 'yogurt culture'. Fermentation of the lactose in the milk by these bacteria produces lactic acid, which acts on the milk protein to give yogurt its texture and its characteristic flavour. So now you know!

There are two main types of yogurt: set and stirred. Set yogurt results when the incubation / fermentation of the milk takes place in the final container / packaging in which it is sold. Stirred yogurt, however, is produced after fermentation has been carried out in bulk, prior to final cooling and packaging.

You can make either plain or natural yogurt, fruit yogurt (by adding fruit and sweeteners) or flavoured yogurt (synthetic flavours and colours).

Frozen yogurt is made in the same way as for the more common refrigerated kind, but it is then deep-frozen to -20°C (and it might need more sugar and stabiliser to withstand the freezer temperatures).

The yogurt culture is usually made up of *Lactobacillus* and *Streptococcus* bacteria. However, you don't have to start growing the bacteria yourself (!); you can buy it or use a commercially-produced yogurt as a convenient source of starter bacteria. Generally, a mixture of *Streptococcus* and *Lactobacillus* has been used to produce the yogurt and are still present in the starter.

The milk is first heated to 90°C to kill any undesirable bacteria and to denature the milk proteins so that they set together rather than form curds. The milk is then cooled to about 40 to 43°C for incubation (or you can cool it completely and reheat it later). The bacteria culture is then added, and the temperature is maintained for four to seven hours to allow fermentation. If you are adding fruit or flavours, add them after fermentation. Altogether, preparation time for a small batch at home in your kitchen can take six to eight hours (or overnight). You can find recipes and procedures for making yogurt in recipe books and elsewhere. Of course, you can buy a yogurt-making machine too!

The ingredients for a typical 500g batch of plain yogurt are:

- 500ml whole pasteurised milk;
- 25g dried milk powder (optional);
- 3 tbsp (75g) live, plain whole-milk yogurt – *starter culture*.

The ingredients costs for this 500g batch are:

	€
Milk (a litre of milk costs around €0.30 if buying direct from farm or €0.80 from a shop)	0.15 / 0.40
Good plain yogurt costs about €0.50/100g, 75g required as starter culture	€0.375
Total cost for ingredients per 500g batch	**€0.525 / 0.775**

Case Study – Yogurt

Velvet Cloud

Rockfield Dairy is owned and run by Michael and Aisling Flanagan and is a sheep dairy business based in Co. Mayo in the West of Ireland, producing milk, yogurt and cheese under the brand Velvet Cloud **(www.velvetcloud.ie)**. "Sheep's milk has a higher nutritional value than cow or goat,

and suits people who may be intolerant to cow's milk. It has a naturally sweeter creamier taste than cow or goat", says Aisling.

Velvet Cloud was awarded a Euro-toque 2016 Food Award for *Innovation in Dairy*, a Silver medal for Velvet Cloud Sheep's Milk in the 2016 Blas na hÉireann awards, Best Newcomer in 2016 by the McKenna Guides, and features on the menu of several of Ireland's Michelin Star restaurants. You can buy Velvet Cloud yogurt (and soon cheese also!)

in speciality food stores, health food stores and in SuperValu. It's also much sought after by chefs in the high-end restaurant and hotel sectors.

Some other yogurt producers include:

- Clandeboye Estate, Co. Down (**www.clandeboye.co.uk**);
- Glenilen Farm, Drimoleague, Co. Cork (**www.glenilenfarm.com**);
- Glenisk cow and goats' milk yogurts, Killeigh, Co. Offaly (**www.glenisk.com**);
- Irish Yogurts, Clonakilty, West Cork (**www.irish-yogurts.ie**);
- Killowen Farm Yogurt, Courtnacuddy, Co. Wexford (**www.killowen.ie**);
- Woodlands Dairy, Dorset, England (**www.woodlandsdairy.co.uk**).

Case Study – Kefir

Blakes Always Organic

Fermented foods are getting lots of attention these days, not least because of their taste, and also because their proponents believe that they are healthier than other foods. One of these – kefir – is a fermented drink that originated in the Middle East and is thought to contribute to a healthy immune system. It is traditionally made using cow or goat's milk. Over a period of time, the microorganisms that are naturally present in the kefir 'grains' multiply and ferment the lactose sugars in the milk into lactic acid, so kefir tastes a bit sour, like a natural yogurt.

Blakes Always Organic (**www.blakesalwaysorganic.ie**) is based in the Food Hub in Drumshanbo, Co. Leitrim and is owned by John Brennan and Sean McGloin, both of whom have worked in the organic sector for many years. Apart from kefir, Blake's also offers organic coffee and organic chocolate and is planning to launch a locally-produced cheese and a kefir and oat product and other varieties in 2017.

Adding Value

As well as cheese, ice cream, yogurt and kefir, other dairy products have emerged over the past few years, including frozen yogurt (**www.chillymoo.ie**), traditional butter like Abernethy Butter in Co. Down (**www.abernethybuttercompany.com**) and Donnybrewer Butter in Derry (**www.donnybrewerbutter.com**), flavoured (black pepper, garlic, sea salt) or herb butters from Improper Butter (**www.improperbutter.com**) and Country Butter, such as Cuinneog.

Case Study – Country Butter

Cuinneog

Cuinneog, the Irish word for churn, was established in 1990 by Tom and Sheila Butler and is run today by their daughter Breda. Production of country butter and buttermilk started in the family kitchen using techniques dating back over 2,000 years. As demand started to grow, the garage was converted into a state-of-the-art food facility and the wooden churn has been replaced by a stainless steel churn but the process remains true to tradition; the cream is fermented and it is this process that gives Cuinneog its distinctive flavour.

Registration

As for all food producers, dairy producers must be registered with DAFM (RoI) or Council (UK/NI).

In the Republic, anyone who wants to make a dairy product or process milk for direct human consumption must contact the Dairy Hygiene Division (057 869 4355 / **dairyhygiene@agriculture.gov.ie**) within DAFM, which will provide further details on the registration/approval process, including application forms and an information pack. This pack includes copies of the relevant legislation and has a requirement for a TB Control Plan (for goats' milk and other non-bovine milk producers), as well as information on all other aspects of milk and dairy production.

Raw Milk

Pasteurisation of milk destroys harmful bacteria but may also destroy nutrients present naturally in the milk. For example, there is some evidence that raw milk may be beneficial for asthma sufferers. Restrictions on the sale of raw milk mean that, provided a raw milk producer is selling less than 30L per week within a 20km radius, then it can be sold directly to the consumer or through shops. If raw milk is used to make a raw cows' milk product, the producer must inform their inspector as to where s/he is sourcing the milk, as herds providing raw milk for the production of raw milk product are subject to two TB tests annually.

Goats' Milk Products

Goats' cheese is everywhere on menus. Apart from the great flavour of goats' milk (though not for everybody!) and goats' cheese, many people choose these foods because goats' milk is often associated with some health benefits, particularly in the case of asthma and eczema. Application for registration and approval for production is made in the normal way.

Anyone who is considering becoming a new entrant to cheese, yogurt or ice cream production is best advised to think carefully. Dairy production is not for the faint hearted, not least because of the costs and legislation involved and the competition in the market.

Training Providers

Cheese-making

Courses for both soft and hard cheese-making are available from:

- CAFRE in Northern Ireland (**www.cafre.ac.uk**);
- Food Industry Training Unit, University College Cork (**www.ucc.ie/fitu**);
- National Organic Training Skillnet, open to non-organic producers also (**www.nots.ie**);
- Teagasc, Moorepark Food Research Centre, Fermoy: Three-day course (**www.teagasc.ie**);

- The Organic Centre: Instructors: Hans and Gaby Wieland. Cost
  €155. Claims to be the only such course in the country covering all
  aspects of cheese-making including cultures, equipment and
  facilities. (**www.theorganiccentre.ie**).

Producers offering training courses include:

- Knockdrinna: A one-day cheese-making course where you make
  your own cheese in the morning, enjoy lunch and then take your
  handmade creation home for maturing. For those in the catering
  industry or interested food production for a living, Helen Finnegan
  is currently designing a professional cheese-making guidance
  course (**www.knockdrinna.com**);
- Silke Croppe at Corleggy Cheeses (**www.corleggycheeses.com**).

Ice Cream-making

Providers include:

- CAFRE in Co. Tyrone, Northern Ireland (**www.cafre.ac.uk**);
- Carpigiani UK Ltd: An Italian ice cream equipment manufacturer,
  providing high quality equipment and services, which runs ice
  cream-making courses in Bologna and the UK
  (**www.gelatouniversity.com**);
- Food Industry Training Unit, University College Cork: *Ice Cream
  Science and Technology* course (fee €1,200). This intensive three-day
  course provides participants with knowledge of the production,
  science, technology, and quality features of frozen desserts, ice
  cream and related products (**www.ucc.ie/fitu**);
- RSS Ltd: The *Introduction to Artisan Ice Cream and Fruit Ice* course is
  suited to newcomers to the world of ice cream and gives a good
  overview of what is required to have your own ice cream business.
  RSS also organises a more advanced course with an Italian chef,
  either in Italy or in Hereford, UK (**www.rsshereford.co.uk**);
- Servequip: Now running a one-day training course once a month,
  showcasing the latest equipment from Frigomat. This course also
  will keep you updated on all the latest industry ideas and trends
  (**www.servequip.co.uk**);

- The Ice Cream Alliance in the UK (**www.ice-cream.org**).

Yogurt-making
Providers here include:

- AB Cheesemaking (UK): Yogurt-making courses, cost £456, payable in full on application (**www.abcheesemaking.co.uk**);
- Ballymaloe Cookery School: Yogurt, butter and cheese-making (**www.cookingisfun.ie**);
- CAFRE (**www.cafre.ac.uk**);
- National Organic Training Skillnet: Yogurt and butter-making – €200 for three-day course (**www.nots.ie**);
- The Organic Centre: Cheese and yogurt courses, prices approx. €140 (**www.theorganiccentre.ie**).

Equipment and Ingredients Suppliers
Note: Prices can vary from a few hundred €/£ to up to €/£5k depending on size, make, capacity.

Cheese Equipment Suppliers

- ALPMA (UK): Specialists in equipment for cheese-making and packaging (**www.alpma.co.uk**);
- C. van't Riet Dairy Technology BV (**www.rietdairy.nl/?lid=2**);
- Jongia (**www.jongia.com**);
- Moorlands Cheesemakers (**www.cheesemaking.co.uk**);
- Old McDonald's Farm & Feed Store (**www.oldmcdonald.ie**);
- Rademaker BV (**www.rademaker.com**);
- Specialist Cheesemakers Association (**www.specialistcheesemakers.co.uk**).

If you are making a small amount of fresh cheese such as cottage- or curd-style cheese, natural live yogurt provides an ideal starter culture. You can also buy freeze-dried varieties.

The following companies offer a mail order service on cheese-making equipment:

- Fullwood Ltd. (**www.fullwood.com**);
- Goat Nutrition Ltd. (**www.gnltd.co.uk**);
- Moorlands Cheesemakers (**www.cheesemaking.co.uk**);
- Stratton Sales (USA) (**wwwstrattonsales.com**).

Yogurt Supplies

- Cloverhill Food Ingredients Ltd (**www.cloverhill.ie**);
- Old McDonald's Farm & Feed Store (**www.oldmcdonald.ie**).

Ice Cream-making Supplies

- Alfred & Co. (UK): Distributor of equipment from WCB Ice Cream, Technogel and Pancolini, covering brand names such as Crepaco, Glacier, Technohoy, Vitaline, PMS, Promco, Grafton and Anderson, all of whom are well regarded in the industry (**www.alfredandco.com**);
- Ashwood Trade Products (UK) (**www.ashwood.biz**);
- Cater Link (UK) (**www.caterlink.co.uk**);
- Dairyglen (**www.dairyglen.ie**) in Bray, Co. Wicklow;
- Martin Food Equipment (**www.martinfoodequip.com**);
- Nisbets: Supply both domestic and small commercial scale equipment (**www.nisbets.ie**).

Other Suppliers

- *DoneDeal* and *Buy & Sell* lists second hand equipment and ice cream carts for sale; and there are many commercial machines listed for sale on eBay (**www.donedeal.ie** or **www.buyandsell.ie**);
- Old McDonald's Farm & Feed Store (**www.oldmcdonald.ie**);
- Robot Coupe (**www.robotcoupe.co.uk**).

Useful Resources

- AB Cheesemaking (UK) (**www.abcheesemaking.co.uk**);
- Cáis, the Association of Irish Farmhouse Cheese-makers (**www.irishcheese.ie**);

- *Dairy Microbiology* by RK Robinson (1981) – an old text, but regarded as the definitive guide;
- DairyCo publication, *On-farm Small-scale Cheese-making: A Beginner's Guide* (**www.dairyco.org.uk**);
- Department of Agriculture, Environment and Rural Affairs (NI) (**www.daera-ni.gov.uk**);
- DAFM (**www.agriculture.gov.ie**);
- *Manufacturing Yogurt and Fermented Milks* by RC Chandan, Blackwell Publishing;
- *Microbiology and Technology of Fermented Foods* by RW Hutkins (2006);
- *On-farm Processing: A Beginner's Guide*: Published in 2007 by the Milk Development Council (UK), it gives a broad point of reference for those considering the manufacture of their own dairy products and can be downloaded free from **www.dairyco.org.uk**;
- Slow Food Ireland: Irish Raw Milk Cheese Presidium (**www.slowfoodireland.com**);
- Society of Dairy Technology (**www.sdt.org**);
- Teagasc (**www.teagasc.ie**);
- The Cheese Hub: Offers cheese ripening and maturing facilities in Co. Leitrim (**www.thecheesehub.ie**);
- The Cheese Web (**www.thecheeseweb.com**);
- The Ice Cream Alliance (UK) (**www.ice-cream.org**).

14

FLESH, FISH AND FOWL

It's hard to beat a good sausage, with smooth mash, gravy and fried onions! In this chapter, we look at how best to approach the development of a range of value-added raw meats including sausages, pies and other foods. The information is relevant for farmers producing livestock, butchers, who may or may not have their own supply of meat, and other food producers who are neither farmers nor butchers.

Consumer Trends

There is no doubt that consumers still enjoy traditional-style meals with meat at the centre (with apologies to vegetarians). The appeal of everyday products that serve up a touch of premium remains popular. An opportunity presents itself for butchers and producers of meat-based foods to meet this demand.

A number of butchers are now producing good quality value-added meat products like sausages, stir fries and casserole mixes, with several other pig, beef and lamb farmers producing some prepared joints, but perhaps not adding value beyond that due to lack of skills and / or facilities. We're talking more than Chicken Maryland or Chicken Kiev here by the way – I think we've moved beyond breadcrumb coating at this stage! Salami, black and white puddings, beef jerky, cured meats, air dried meats, venison sausages – all have emerged over the past few years.

Trends in the sector include meatballs in sauce, stuffed joints with raw vegetables in tray, straight-to-oven, smoked sausages and premium sausages (with at least 80% meat). Cornish pasties and old-fashioned meat pies have made a bit of a comeback also. There is always a demand from consumers for good quality, locally-produced, value-added meat products that provide a 'meal solution'.

Working in co-operation with other producers can be very useful – for example, the local butcher supplying meat to local pasty-maker, who then sells their ready-to-cook pasties in the butcher's shop. Selling value-added foods through butcher shops that have supplied the meat is a really good way to co-operate, each promoting the other.

Breed branding is becoming a more common feature, with breeds such as Angus and Wagyu (Kobe) becoming better known, along with Dexter and Irish Moiled beef. Be sure to promote the quality of the meat from the breed, especially if it is niche or already has good brand recognition. Angus beef's association with quality is well-known and is positioned as a cut above 'ordinary' beef. Brands within retail and food service are increasingly playing on consumers' apparent growing appreciation of Angus beef.

The range of potential value-added products includes:

- Sausages;
- Steak burgers;
- Oven ready meals – stuffed joints with or without vegetables;
- Stir fries with sauce and/or vegetables;
- Casserole mixes (with vegetables);
- Meatballs in tomato sauce;
- Pasties and pies.

How to Make Sausages

The production of value-added meat products has evolved from kitchen to butcher to factory. However, the quality of the meat, the key ingredient, is important in terms of producing flavour and eating quality.

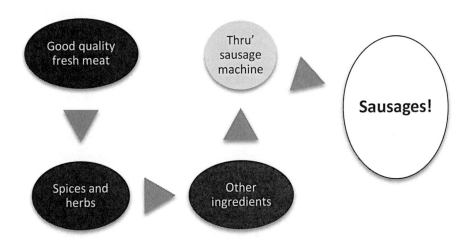

Sausage Casings

The choice of sausage casings is between natural or synthetic.

Natural casings are more expensive and tricky to work with. Natural casings are generally made from the intestines of the animal and are cleaned, bleached and preserved in salt and so these must be soaked in cold water before use (preferably overnight). Fresh casings have a shelf life of about two months if kept in salt and kept refrigerated. Natural casings are the only casings that can be used in organic sausage production.

Other casings can be vegetarian, synthetic or made from collagen. They have a much longer shelf life than natural casings and often do not need to be refrigerated. Once these casings have been filled, it is important that the sausages are left in the refrigerator overnight to rest. The herbs and spices marinate with the meat and the skins rehydrate. These skins look and feel just like normal skins, and are often less 'chewy' than fresh casings. For more information, contact the International Natural Sausage Casing Association (**www.insca.org**).

Processing Partners

Unless you are already a butcher, you'll need access to or to partner with a butcher who can offer you good quality cutting and production facilities. You might not be able to afford to buy a sausage-making machine straight away, but perhaps your local friendly butcher would make the sausages or burgers for you, to your recipe, if you ask nicely!

Production Requirements

Producing raw or cooked meat products in the kitchen at home isn't really feasible. Meat products are considered to be high-risk, so there is no avoiding a dedicated place in which to prepare your foods.

If you are planning to make cooked meats, then you must have physically-separated raw and cooked areas. This is no small undertaking and should not be entered into lightly. It simply cannot be done at home.

For raw meat products, what you will need is a combination of some or all of the following:

- Suitable dedicated approved premises;
- Dedicated preparation area;
- Store for dry ingredients and for packaging;
- Sausage machine, mincing and mixing machines, knives, chopping boards and so on;
- A packaging area where the finished product is weighed and packed;
- A cold room to store the packaged product.

The capital costs of building and equipping a medium-sized facility (1,250 sq. ft.) might be as much as €100,000 if you are starting from scratch, assuming you have a site already. Conversion of an existing garage or other premises may be cheaper, though it depends on the conversion work that needs to be done. Equipment costs vary and are available from the suppliers listed at the end of this chapter.

Nonetheless, the word on the street is that margins on sausages are very high, and that they are a valuable product for butchers – see more below.

Smoked Meat and Fish

If you plan to set up a smokehouse for producing smoked meat or fish, special consideration must be given to buying the unsmoked foods from a reliable source, obtaining the appropriate test results and ensuring that your supplier complies with all the relevant legislative and hygiene requirements.

Cold Smoking

Cold smoking is one of the oldest-known preservation methods. However, smoking of foods today is usually done for the flavour rather than for preservation. While the smoke is an anti-microbial and anti-oxidant, it is not sufficient for preserving food in practice, unless combined with another preservation method such as salt-curing or drying.

Cold smoking allows total smoke penetration into the side of the meat. Very little hardening of the outside surface of the meat (casing) occurs and smoke penetrates the meat easily. Cold smoking prevents or slows down the spoilage of fats, which increases their shelf life. Cold smoked products are not submitted to any heat and so are not cooked.

Some important points to remember:

- Cold smoking is carried out typically at temperatures between 10°C and 32°C;
- Only use containers that are made from either food-grade plastic or high-quality stainless steel for preparing meats;
- Don't use woods that have been treated, or come from an unknown source;
- Using dry wood is of utmost importance when cold smoking.

Smoked salmon is smoked with cold smoke for an extended period of time. Applying hotter smoke (over 28°C) will cook the fish – sometimes sold as 'barbequed salmon' – changing the flavour and making it more difficult to slice it as thinly as the cold smoked version.

Cold smoking is a slow process. Hams, which lend themselves perfectly to this type of smoking, can be smoked from two to even six weeks. During smoking, they will slowly acquire a golden colour along with a smoky flavour.

Hot Smoking

Hot smoking dries out the surface of the meat, creating a barrier for smoke penetration. Although foods that have been hot smoked are often reheated or cooked, they are typically safe to eat without further cooking. Typical temperatures used are in the range of 52°C to 80°C.

Food Safety and Other Legislation

There are specific considerations to be taken into account when working with smoked fish. *Listeria monocytogenes* can survive at refrigeration temperatures and sometimes can be associated with food poisoning from smoked fish. The Sea Fisheries Protection Authority has produced a useful leaflet that can be downloaded from **www.sfpa.ie**. It is necessary for food producers who sell to the public to be registered with the HSE, as described already in **Chapter 3**.

Specific legislation applies to the use and declaration of smoke flavourings. The Environmental Protection Agency (**www.epa.ie**) advises that *Air Quality Regulations* for the smoke house may apply.

The Economics of Making Sausages

Let's look at making sausages, considering the various stages in the process separately to identify the costs and margins:

- **Supplier of raw materials:** Butcher or yourself if you have a farm;
- **Producer:** Butcher or sausage-maker;
- **Retailer:** Shop.

The butcher buys pigs for €25 per pig. Each results in 25kg of meat (€1/kg), which he sells for €2/kg.

Product	Direct Costs	Selling Price	Simple Gross Profit (SGP)	Simple Gross Margin (SGM)
	(a)	(b)	(c= b –a)	(d = c/bx100)
Meat	€1	€2	€1	50%

The sausage-maker makes 1.5kg of sausage from 1kg of meat, which he sells for €4.50/kg. Labour cost is not included here, but all other ingredients cost €1.

Product	Direct Costs /kg (a)	Selling Price (b)	SGP (c= b −a)	SGM (d = c/bx100)
Sausages	€3	€4.50	€1.50	33%

The retailer sells the sausages for €8/kg; his/her direct cost is the purchase price s/he paid the sausage-maker.

Product	Direct Costs (a)	Selling Price (b)	SGP (c = b − a)	SGM (d=c/bx100)
Sausages	€4.50	€8	€3.50	44%

The Simple Gross Margin (SMG) in the chain shows:

- The butcher 50%;
- The processor 33%;
- The shop 44%.

Margins are highest for the butcher selling just meat, then the shop-owner who sells sausages and lowest for the sausage-maker. If the butcher makes and sells the sausages direct to the public, margins improve further.

Product	Direct Costs (a)	Selling Price (b)	SGP (c =b −a)	SGM (d = c/bx100)
Sausages	€2	€8	€6	75%

By presenting the margins in this way, you can see at a glance where the greatest margins (and so the best way to make the most money) lie. It shows how a producer can add value to meat.

Case Studies

The following are some good examples of the high standards that can be achieved by small producers. Note how each has personalised their business and promotes tradition and provenance as a unique selling point (USP).

Coopershill Venison

Coopershill in Co. Sligo has been in the O'Hara family since it was built in 1774, with the 8th generation now calling it home. Approximately 200 fallow deer roam the fields at Coopershill and are grass-fed throughout spring and summer. Mother and son, the inimitable Lindy and Simon, encourage farm visits so that consumers of Coopershill Venison can see first-hand the

importance that they attach to the animals' welfare (**www.coopershill.com/venison.html**).

The advantage of farmed over wild venison is that they know the exact age of each animal and therefore can guarantee flavour and tenderness of the meat. High in iron and a plethora of vitamins, very lean and low in saturated fat, venison is the perfect red meat for anyone who cares about their cholesterol levels but still enjoys an exquisite meal.

Jack and Eddie's Sausages

The O'Malley family farm has been in existence for five generations. Jack is the fifth generation

and Eddie, Jack's dad, is the fourth. The farm is nestled in the hills between Westport in Co. Mayo and Leenane, Co. Galway. Eddie is a farmer at heart but has always been concerned with the difficulty of making a living from farming. With many locals interested in tasting the produce, Eddie decided to start making sausages, which allows him to continue to make a living from the farm (**www.jackandeddies.com**). Jack and Eddie use a secret family recipe for their sausages and a traditional cure for rashers from only the best cuts of pork. They have recently launched a new range of black and white puddings.

Smoked Meat – Ummera Smokehouse

In the early 1970s, Anthony Creswell's father, a keen fisherman, started smoking the salmon he and his friends were catching on the local rivers, the Argideen, the Bandon, and the Blackwater. After much trial and error, he perfected the method of smoking salmon, which remain unchanged today. Anthony took over the running of the company from his father in 1998. Over nearly 40 years, Ummera **(www.ummera.com)** has built up an enviable reputation for producing some of the finest Irish organic smoked salmon available.

The vitality of fine quality food producers in the West Cork area helps the Ummera Smokehouse to maintain a vibrancy and high level of interest, maintaining quality and continually developing expertise. Ummera smoked products (including smoked eel, smoked chicken, smoked duck and smoked dry cured bacon – with no artificial preservatives) are available at a range of outlets in Ireland, and also for direct sales from the smokehouse. Most recently, Anthony has launched smoked Irish Organic Picanha beef, which, I can tell you, is absolutely delicious!

Smoked Salmon – Burren Smokehouse

The award-winning Burren Smokehouse **(www.burrensmokehouse.ie)** is a family-run artisan producer of smoked  salmon products, set up in 1989 by Birgitta and Peter Curtin in Lisdoonvarna, Co. Clare. The smokehouse supplies to high-end customers within the deli, restaurant and retail sector worldwide. All the salmon is 100% Irish and organic. Varieties include cold smoked salmon, honey glazed cold smoked salmon with honey, whiskey and fennel (absolutely delicious!), as well as smoked salmon with seaweed, very on-trend! A Visitor Centre was established in 1995, to create a window for Burren Smokehouse's own range and other local gourmet products and crafts. It has become a popular tourist attraction in the North County Clare area and welcomes over 30,000 visitors from all over the world each year.

West Cork Pies

When Paul Phillips moved to West Cork, he couldn't find a pork pie anywhere, so he decided to start making and selling them himself – a perfect example of a food business filling a local demand! He started with a market stall and the business grew from there. All their prime

Schull ★ West Cork

ingredients – the meat, eggs and vegetables – are sourced from local farmers in West Cork, in most cases direct from the farmer him/herself, and the Phillips rear their own traditional breed pigs which are used for their pork-based products. In addition to pork pies, West Cork Pies (**www.westcorkpies.com**) has expanded its range to include artisan pies, ready-to-eat meals and snacks. With Great Taste and Blas na hÉireann awards under their belts, West Cork Pies are available in supermarkets nationwide.

Equipment Suppliers

Equipment can be purchased from a number of suppliers, who often offer training courses and can provide a great deal of technical and other advice. Prices can vary from a few hundred € to up to €5,000, depending on size, make, capacity, etc. Suppliers include:

- Brennan Group (**www.brennan-group.com**);
- *Buy & Sell* lists second hand equipment for sale (**www.buyandsell.ie**);
- Macs BBQ (UK) (**www.macsbbq.co.uk**);
- Martin Food Equipment (**www.martinfoodequip.com**);
- McDonnell's Ltd (**www.mcdonnells.ie**);
- Nisbets supply both domestic and small commercial scale equipment (**www.nisbets.ie**);

- Old McDonald's Farm & Feed Store (**www.oldmcdonald.ie**);
- Robot Coupe (**www.robotcoupe.co.uk**);
- Scobie & Junor (Dublin) Ltd. (**www.scobiesdirect.com**);
- Smoky Jo's Cooking School (UK) (**www.smokyjos.co.uk**).

Ingredient Suppliers

- Brennan Group (**www.brennan-group.com**);
- CaterPac: For packaging (**www.caterpac.ie**);
- CF Gaynor Ltd: For marinades, sauces, herbs and spices, sausage mixes and coatings (**www.cfgaynor.com**);
- Irish Casing Company Ltd: For casings (**www.irishcasings.com**);
- McDonnell's Ltd (**www.mcdonnells.ie**);
- Scobie & Junor (Dublin) Ltd. (**www.scobiesdirect.com**).

Useful Resources

- Campden BRI (UK) (**www.campden.co.uk**);
- DAFM (**www.agriculture.gov.ie**);
- Leatherhead Food Research (UK) (**www.leatherheadfood.com**);

Training Providers

- Andrew Chilton: Sausage-making course includes food safety; history of sausages; sausage-making process; recipes and practical sausage-making;
- Associated Craft Butchers of Ireland: Offers butchery training coupled with a recognised FETAC Level 5 qualification specific to butchery (**www.craftbutchers.ie**);
- Butchery classes at James McGeough Butchers (**www.connemarafinefoods.ie**);
- Butchery classes at James Whelan Butchers (**www.jameswhelanbutcher.com**);
- CAFRE (**www.cafre.ac.uk**);
- Dublin Institute of Technology, School of Culinary Arts & Food Technology: Sometimes runs courses in collaboration with the

Associated Craft Butchers of Ireland
(**www.dit.ie/culinaryartsandfoodtechnology/**);

- Food Industry Training Unit, College of Science, Engineering and Food Science, University College Cork (**www.ucc.ie/fitu**);
- National Organic Training Skillnet (NOTS): Sausage-making courses; butchery and small scale meat production: course covers the factors affecting the quality of meat; meat presentation / the potential uses of the various cuts of meat; labelling issues; handling of meat – food safety issues; bacon-curing and smoking – one-day course on wet and dry curing and smoking (**www.nots.ie**);
- Pat O'Doherty in Enniskillen, Co. Fermanagh is famous for his Black Bacon brand; he also offers training (**www.blackbacon.com**);
- Skillnets: Some Skillnets may have relevant courses (**www.skillnets.ie**) - for example, Taste 4 Success Skillnet (**www.taste4success.ie**);
- Teagasc, Ashtown: Meat Hygiene, FETAC Level 5 – course covers animal welfare relating to slaughter; red meat slaughter procedure and hygiene controls; anatomy and physiology of farm animals; nutrition, growth and metabolism of farm animals; basic pathology and disease; post-mortem inspection procedures; food-borne illnesses and zoonoses; meat processing; the red meat industry – summary and future (**www.teagasc.ie**);
- Teagasc: Butchery and meat management, food safety, labelling and more (**www.teagasc.ie**);

Smoked Foods Courses

- Old Smokehouse Foods & Equipment (UK) (**www.the-old-smokehouse.co.uk**);
- Smallholding Ireland, **www.smallholding.ie**;
- Smoky Jo's Cooking School (UK) (**www.smokyjos.co.uk**).

15

WHAT ELSE IS NEW?

Dips, chocolate, salts and drinks – and a bit of whatever you fancy!

In addition to bread, cakes, jam, eggs, ice cream, yogurt, cheese and meat, there are so many other possibilities for small food producers – chocolate, fudge, chutney, dips, flavoured vinegar, flavoured salt, sea salt, marshmallows, popcorn, macaroons, rapeseed oil, salads, mashed vegetables, granola, prepared sandwiches, crisps, snails, pizza, cake and bread mixes, and we haven't even touched drinks! Craft beer, gin, elderflower and other cordials, fruit juice, vegetable juice, wheatgrass, smoothies, kombucha, green tea drinks, tea blenders, coffee roasters, the list is literally endless!

So, to give you some inspiration and an idea of the potential possibilities, I've selected a few case studies for you to enjoy.

Case Studies

Achill Island Sea Salt

When I first met Marjorie O'Malley in 2013, and she described how they had started hand-harvesting seawater from the Atlantic Ocean to produce sea salt in open pans in their
kitchen, I asked her, "Why?". She answered, "Because it's great fun, it's exciting!"… and hard work too I'm sure, but it certainly is worth it! The O'Malley family has revived the industry of salt production on Achill Island, which existed back in the 1800s.

This multi-award-winning sea salt is literally the softest salt you will try, the flakes dissolve in front of your eyes. It has lower sodium than other salts and a high mineral content with over 60 naturally-occurring trace elements. As well all that, it adds really great flavour. No wonder chefs love it! Achill Island Sea Salt (**www.achillislandseasalt.ie**) is available in good shops all across the country.

Cabot's of Westport

Redmond Cabot has had a varied career – from being a photographer, then a retailer,

CABOTS OF WESTPORT

a restaurateur, through being unemployed, surviving the recession, becoming a father and finally launching his new food business in 2012, which has gone from strength to strength. His energy and enthusiasm for his work cannot but have an effect on the people he meets. When Red describes the beetroot and sage dip, the chilli hummus, the smoked trout pâté, and the black olive tapenade he makes, your mouth will water – I guarantee it! He'll talk about how he roasts the chilli peppers himself because it brings out the heat better, and how you will notice the flavour of the sage coming through at the end as you enjoy the beetroot and sage dip. He's a great salesman talking honestly about his high-quality, hand-made food, which is available in Supervalu and good shops everywhere between Westport and Dublin.

Mash Direct

Martin and Tracy Hamilton are vegetable farmers. However, making money from growing vegetables was proving challenging and in 2003, over a glass of whiskey after a dinner party, Martin decided he'd start to mash his spuds and make champ, a traditional

Ulster vegetable dish. They set up a small production unit, and since

then, with lots of hard work and determination, the business has grown fast. From selling at St. George's Market in Belfast and local shops, Mash Direct is now available in supermarket multiples across Ireland and the UK and employs over 200 staff! The production site is gluten-free and the multi-award winning range includes vegetables that are diced, sliced, chopped, shredded, steamed and fried into everything from neeps and tatties (look it up!) to veggie burgers (another of my personal favourites). You just have to try their carrot and parsnip fries!

Rafferty's Fine Foods

Rafferty's Fine Foods was established by chef Declan Rafferty in the seaside village of Blackrock, Co. Louth. Declan wanted to make his own range of top quality, flavoursome homemade chutney, relishes, marinades, flavoured oils,  infused sea salt flakes, dressings and jams. He has succeeded in doing just that and has several Great Taste and Blas na hÉireann awards to prove it! I use the chilli-infused oil all the time for stir fries and the lemon and lime-infused sea salt when cooking fish, or just anything else for that matter! The rosemary and mint salt is great with lamb, of course. The range is available in Supervalu and other shops across the country.

Blanco Nino

BLANCO NIÑO   BLANCO NIÑO

The story of Blanco Niño began with Philip Martin's frustration in not being able to find real corn tortillas in Europe. It led to him travelling to the farms, mills and tortilla factories of Mexico to learn the process, history and cultural importance behind the art of making tortillas. His learnings on this trip emboldened Philip to launch what was a hugely successful crowdfunding campaign (check it out on YouTube). Following this, he assembled an experienced management team, launched the Tortilleria in Clonmel, Co. Tipperary and is now selling across Ireland, the UK, Germany, Luxembourg, Finland, the Netherlands, France and Spain.

Richmount Elderflower Cordial

Could anyone have possible predicted the rise of the elderflower? I don't think so, and yet in Longford, David and Martina Burns set about planting their farm with elderflower with a view to setting up a cordial company. David had been farming on the family farm since 1977. Martina was a primary school principal and had been making elderflower cordial for home use for years. David asked a few restaurant chefs to sample it and, based on their reaction and the encouragement of friends, the idea of commercial elderflower cordial production was born. After lots of tweaking, they finally decided on "Special Recipe No. 9". In January 2013, the Richmount Cordial Company (**www.richmountcordials.ie**) was formed. David and Martina planted 920 elder saplings and are now producing small batches of award-winning elderflower cordial. If you're fond of a gin and tonic, then take my advice and try it with a dash of Richmount Elderflower Cordial, I promise you won't be disappointed!

The Cultured Club

Dearbhla Reynolds, based in Belfast, is founder of The Cultured Club, an umbrella organisation for all things fermented (**www.theculturedclub.com**). Her passion for these foods started with an article about probiotic ketchup, which quickly escalated into a love affair, with many different fermentation experiments to follow and a laboratory-like kitchen. There is such a range of fermented foods, all of which are bursting with flavour, nutrients and life.

To pick a favourite would be difficult as each aspect of this lost skill really offers so much more than merely a new flavour or different taste. Kimchi would definitely feature as a palate teaser but, for the uninitiated, fermenting your salsa will win over any tastebuds. Dearbhla says that fermentation offers all of life's pleasures and a glass of fizzy, traditionally fermented lemonade is something you just cannot believe is good for you! Dearbhla published her book *The Cultured Club – Fabulously Funky Fermentation Recipes* in 2016.

Mallow Mia

Linda McClean, originally from Derry in Northern Ireland, brought many years of sound scientific knowledge and experience in the food industry to her new food business, Mallow Mia, which she set up in Donegal in 2014 and won Gold at Blas na hÉireann in 2015. Linda makes luxuriously light

handcrafted marshmallows, in the most delicious flavours – lemon meringue, raspberry, coconut, white chocolate and many more, all wonderful. She sells at events and fair and also makes personalised wedding favours.

KooKee

Pauline Clarke's love of baking started from a very early age and her years working within food manufacturing has given her

valuable inside knowledge of how to run a successful artisan bakery. The inspiration for KooKee came after spending Saturday mornings baking cookies with her three children. She had given up work to become a carer for her eldest son, who was diagnosed with a form of autism. Saturdays became a ritual baking day, involving all the children in a fun family task.

After many weeks and lots of cookies, Pauline and her children started giving them as gifts to family and friends. Over the next few months, Pauline perfected her recipes and decided that this would be a wonderful way to care for her kids and make her hobby into a business. So, in 2009, she registered KooKee (**www.kookee.ie**) and tried out her products at local farmers' markets and craft fairs. Pauline says that she owes much to the support of her husband and the enthusiasm of her children.

KooKee is going from strength to strength with nine flavours now, including gluten-free and wheat-free varieties, as well as an innovative new dry-mix range that can be adapted by the consumer so that it is suitable not only for gluten-free and wheat-free diets, but also for vegetarians and vegans.

Drumshanbo Gunpowder Gin

How many different types of gin can you name? It used to be about three, now it must be about 33! That said, as with most foods and drinks, some are definitely better than others and this one is simply fabulous. I'd never tasted gin neat before, but was gently persuaded to try this one at the Manorhamilton Agricultural Show a couple of years ago, and I was hooked. Yes, I'm a gin drinker anyway, but this one is special, and I'm not just saying that because it's made in Leitrim! It is made with a range of 12 botanicals, which give it its wonderful flavour. Founder PJ Rigney brought his experience of the drinks industry with him to Leitrim where he set up The Shed Distillery in 2016. Gunpowder Gin (**www.gunpowdergin.com**) is widely available in shops, pubs and restaurants across the land. Try it with some good tonic (Poachers made in Wexford is great – **www.poacherswell.com**) and a dash of Richmount Cordial, see above!

Sweet Beat

Carolanne Rushe used to run the Green Warrior food stall at the Strandhill Market in Sligo. Her plant-based foods quickly earned her a reputation for good, flavoursome, innovative

vegan dishes and her stall sold out regularly. She cultivated a loyal following for her vegan salads, fresh nut milks, and raw treats; the market was the perfect platform to test products on the local market and see whether there was demand.

Trained at Ballymaloe Cookery School in 2013, Carolanne had spent the previous six years travelling and blogged her way around the globe, documenting and sharing recipes and flavours as she discovered them. Following a busy summer season at the market, and when a retail premises became available at the start of 2015, Carolanne jumped at the opportunity to develop a café (**www.sweetbeat.ie**).

In 2016, she launched her retail range, which includes kale pesto, and can be bought in the café as well as in Supervalu stores.

16

WHERE TO NOW? HELP IS AT HAND

Many resources and sources of information have been mentioned throughout the book already. Here they are again, all in one place – along with a few more:

- *365 Social Media Tips: Master Social Media One Day at a Time*, e-book by Lorna Sixsmith and Amanda Webb, on Amazon.
- **AB Cheesemaking**, 7 Daybell Close, Bottesford, Nottingham NG13 0DQ, www.abcheesemaking.co.uk, (01949) 842867.
- **Abernethy Butter**, 66 Ballynahinch Road, Dromara, Co. Down BT25 2AL, www.abernethybuttercompany.com, (078) 9013 9357.
- **About Hygiene Ltd.**, Ballinamore, Co. Leitrim, www.about-hygiene.com, (071) 964 5111.
- **Achill Island Sea Salt, Bunacurry, Achill Island, Co.** Mayo, www.achillislandseasalt.ie, info@achillislandseasalt.ie, (098) 47856.
- **Alfred & Co.**, West Carr Road, Retford, Nottinghamshire DN22 7SN, www.alfredandco.com, info@icecream.alfred.co.uk, (01777) 701141.
- **Alpha Omega Consultants Ltd.**, Dromahair, Co. Leitrim, www.alphaomega.ie, oonagh@alphaomega.ie, (071) 916 4003.
- **ALPMA GB Ltd.**, 1 Devonshire Business Park, Knights Park Road, Basingstoke RG21 6XN, www.alpma.co.uk, info@alpma.co.uk, (01256) 467177.
- **Andrew Chilton**, Boyle, Co. Roscommon, andrew.chilton@gmail.com, (086) 662 7415.
- **Andrews Food Ingredients**, 27 Ferguson Drive, Knockmore Hill Industrial Park, Lisburn, Co. Antrim BT28 2EX, www.andrewingredients.co.uk, leah@andrewingredients.co.uk, (028) 9267 2525.

- **Ashwood Trade Products**, Crown House, Home Gardens, Dartford, Kent DA1 1DZ, www.ashwood.biz, sales@ashwood.biz, (01332) 369000.
- **Associated Craft Butchers of Ireland**, Research Office 1, Ashtown Food Research Centre, Teagasc, Ashtown, Dublin 15, www.craftbutchers.ie, (01) 868 2820.
- **Bakery Bits Ltd.**, 1 Orchard Units, Duchy Road, Honiton, Devon EX14 1YD, www.bakerybits.co.uk, enquiry@bakerybits.co.uk, (01404) 565656.
- **Baldwin's Farmhouse Ice Cream**, Killeenagh, Knockanore, Co. Waterford, www.baldwinsicecream.com, thomas@baldwinsicecream.com, (086) 322 0932.
- **Ballymaloe Cookery School**, Shanagarry, Co. Cork, www.cookingisfun.ie, info@cookingisfun.ie, (021) 464 6785.
- **Bestbreadmachinereviews.com**.
- **Bfree Foods**, 10 Clyde Road, Dublin 4, www.bfreefoods.com, info@bfreefoods.com, (01) 779 0500.
- **Bia at Home**, Ballinrobe Enterprise Centre, Kilmaine Road, Ballinrobe, Co. Mayo, www.biaathome.ie.
- **BigBarn CIC**, College Farm, Great Barford, Bedfordshire MK44 3JJ, www.bigbarn.co.uk, info@bigbarn.co.uk, (01480) 890970.
- **Billy Bob's Pet & Country Superstore**, Unit 4, Cottage Hill, Loughrea, Co. Galway, www.billybobs.ie, (091) 847866.
- **Blakes Always Organic**, Drumshanbo Enterprise Centre, Hill Road, Drumshanbo, Co. Leitrim, www.blakesalwaysorganic.ie, (071) 931 8509.
- **Blanco Niño**, Carrigeen Business Park, Clonmel, Co. Tipperary, www.blanco-nino.com, hello@blanco-nino.com, (052) 618 9723.
- **Blas na hÉireann / National Irish Food Awards**, 10 Emlagh, Dingle, Co. Kerry, www.irishfoodawards.com, info@irishfoodawards.com, (087) 902 9329.
- **Bluebell Falls Ltd.**, Newtownshandrum, Charleville, Co. Cork, www.bluebellfalls.com, info@bluebellfalls.com, (063) 72999.
- **Bord Bia**, Clanwilliam Court, Lower Mount Street, Dublin 2, www.bordbia.ie / www.bordbiavantage.ie, (01) 668 5155.
- **Braemar Farm Ice Cream**, 67 Altikeeragh Road, Castlerock, Coleraine BT51 4ST, (028) 7084 8331.

- **Brandshapers Ltd.**, Ballytramon Business Park, Ardcavan, Castlebridge, Co. Wexford, www.brandshapers.ie, info@brandshapers.ie, (053) 917 7580.
- **Brennan Group**, Cloone, Co. Leitrim, www.brennan-group.com, info@brennan-group.com, (071) 963 6038.
- **Burren Smokehouse**, Kincora Road, Lisdoonvarna, Co. Clare, www.burrensmokehouse.ie, info@burrensmokehouse.ie, (065) 707 4432.
- *Buy & Sell*, www.buyandsell.ie.
- **C. van't Riet Dairy Technology BV**, Energieweg 20, 2421 LM Nieuwkoop, The Netherlands, www.rietdairy.nl/?lid=2, info@rietdairy.nl, (0172) 571304.
- **Cabot's of Westport**, Lanmore, Westport, Co. Mayo, (098) 21932.
- **CAFRE (College of Agriculture, Food and Rural Enterprise)**, Loughry College, Cookstown, Co. Tyrone BT80 9AA, www.cafre.ac.uk, enquiries@cafre.ac.uk, (028) 8676 8101.
- **Cáis**, The Association of Irish Cheese-makers, www.irishcheese.ie.
- **Campden BRI**, Station Road, Chipping Campden, Gloucestershire GL55 6LD, www.campden.co.uk, info@campden.co.uk, (01366) 842000.
- **Cannaboe Confectionery**, Willowfield Road, Ballinamore, Co. Leitrim, www.cacamilis.ie, info@cacamilis.ie, (071) 964 4778.
- **Carpigiani UK Ltd.**, Faculty House, 214 Holme Lacy Road, Hereford HR2 6BQ, www.carpigiani.co.uk, info@carpigiani.co.uk, (01432) 346018.
- **Carrowholly Cheese**, Westport, Co. Mayo, carrowhollycheese@gmail.com, (087) 237 3536.
- **Castlehill Foods**, Carrowmore, Lacken, Killala, Co. Mayo, (096) 34444 / (087) 652 6065.
- **Castlerea Enterprise Hub**, Community & Enterprise Centre, Castlerea, Co. Roscommon, www.castlreaenterprisehub.com.
- **Cater Link**, Units 7-8, Bodmin Business Park, Launceston Road, Bodmin, Cornwall PL31 2RJ, www.caterlink.co.uk, sales@caterlink.co.uk, (01208) 78844.
- **CaterPac @ Scallans Food Service Ltd.**, Whitemill Industrial Estate, Wexford, www.caterpac.ie, (053) 918 4745 / (087) 298 0558 (Sales).

- **CF Gaynor Ltd.**, Unit 19, Hub Logistics Park, Bracetown, Clonee, Dublin 15, www.cfgaynor.com, info@cfgaynor.com, (01) 825 2700.
- **Check out My Buns**, Unit 5, East Belfast Enterprise Park, 308 Albertbridge Road, Belfast BT5 4GX, www.checkoutmybuns.com, (07808) 934518.
- **ChillyMoo Frozen Yogurts**, www.chillymoo.ie, clare@chillymoo.ie / joanna@chillymoo.ie , (086) 858 3800 / (086) 817 4571.
- **Chin Chin Labs**, 49-50 Camden Lock Place, London NW1 8AF, www.chinchinlabs.com, nitro@chinchinlabs.com, (07885) 604284.
- **City Cheese**, 64b Main Street, Ballywalter, Co. Down, www.citycheese.co.uk, swanepeol_c@yahoo.com, (075) 9929 5945.
- **Clandeboye Estate**, Bangor, Co. Down, www.clandeboye.co.uk, courtyard@clandeboye.co.uk, (028) 9185 3457.
- **Cloverhill Food Ingredients Ltd.**, Mountleader Industrial Estate, Millstreet, Co. Cork, www.cloverhill.ie, sales@cloverhill.ie, (029) 21844.
- **Coeliac Society of Ireland**, Carmichael House, 4 North Brunswick Street, Dublin 7, www.coeliac.ie, info@coeliac.ie, (01) 872 1471.
- **Coeliac UK**, 3rd Floor, Apollo Centre, Desborough Road, High Wycombe, Bucks HP11 2QW, www.coeliac.org.uk, (01494) 437278.
- **Connacht Gold**, Tubbercurry, Co. Sligo, www.connachtgold.ie, info@cgold.ie, (071) 918 6500.
- **Coopershill Venison**, Riverstown, Co. Sligo, www.coopershill.com /venison.html, venison@coopershill.com, (087) 792 8789.
- **Cork Incubator Kitchens**, Unit 1 & 2, Street J, Carrigaline Industrial Est., Kilnageary Road, Carrigaline, Co. Cork, www.corkincubatorkitchens.ie, info@corkincubatorkitchens.ie, (087) 623 3088.
- **Corleggy Cheeses**, Belturbet, Co. Cavan, www.corleggycheeses.com.
- **County Dublin Beekeepers' Association**, www.dublinbees.org, info@dublinbees.org.
- **Crossgar Foodservice**, Farranfad Road, Seaforde, Downpatrick, BT30 8NH, Northern Ireland, online.crossgar.ie, sales@crossgar.ie, (028) 4481 1500.
- **Cuinneog**, Balla, Castlebar, Co. Mayo, www.cuinneog.com, info@cuinneog.com, (094) 903 1425.
- *Dairy Microbiology*, book by RK Robinson, John Wiley & Sons.

- **DairyCo**, Agriculture and Horticulture Development Board, Stoneleigh Park, Kenilworth, Warwickshire CV8 2TL, www.dairyco.org.uk, info@dairyco.ahdb.org.uk, (024) 7669 2051.
- **Dairyglen**, Southern Cross Business Park, Bray, Co. Wicklow, www.dairyglen.ie, info@dairyglen.ie, (1890) 200052.
- **Dart Mountain Cheese**, Tamnagh Foods Ltd., 26 Tamnagh Road, Park, Claudy, Co. Derry BT47 4DN, www.dartmountaincheese.com, info@dartmountaincheese.com, (077) 7958 0542.
- **Denise's Delicious**, Unit 17/18, Euro Business Park, Little Island, Cork, www.delicious.ie, (021) 435 5536.
- **Department of Agriculture, Environment and Rural Affairs (NI)**, Dundonald House, Upper Newtownards Road, Ballymiscaw, Belfast BT4 3SB, www.daera-ni.gov.uk, dardhelpline@daera-ni.gov.uk, (028) 9052 4420.
- **Department of Agriculture, Food and the Marine** (DAFM), Agriculture House, Kildare Street, Dublin 2, www.agriculture.gov.ie, info@agriculture.gov.ie, (01) 607 2000.
- **Done Deal**, www.donedeal.ie.
- **Donnybrewer Butter**, 102 Donnybrewer Road, Eglinton, Londonderry BT47 3PE, www.donnybrewerbutter.com, donnybrewerbutter@hotmail.com, (078) 9187 8262.
- **Dozio's of Mayo**, Barroe, Carracastle, Co. Mayo, doziocheese@gmail.com.
- **Dublin Institute of Technology**, School of Culinary Arts and Food Technology, Cathal Brugha Street, Dublin 1, www.dit.ie/culinaryartsandfoodtechnology/.
- **Dunnes Stores**, 46-50 South Great George's Street, Dublin 2, www.dunnestsores.com.
- **Easy Equipment**, 66 Jersey Street, Manchester M4 6JQ, www.easyequipment.ie. sales@easyequipment.ie.
- **Enterprise Ireland**, Eastpoint Business Park, Dublin 3, www.enterprise-ireland.com, (01) 727 2000.
- **Environmental Health Association Ireland**, Heraghty House, 4 Carlton Terrace, Novara Avenue, Bray, Co. Wicklow, www.ehai.ie, (01) 276 1211.
- **Environmental Protection Agency**, PO Box 3000, Johnstown Castle Estate, Wexford, www.epa.ie, (053) 916 0600.

- **Erin Grove Preserves**, 41 Derryhillagh Road, Lissan, Enniskillen, Co. Fermanagh BT74 4DX, www.eringrove.com, hello@eringrove.com, (028) 6632 8206.
- **Euro-toques**, 11 Bridge Court, City Gate, St. Augustine's Street, Galway, www.euro-toques.ie, info@euro-toques.ie, (01) 677 9995.
- **Fabio's Ice Cream & Coffee**, Lower Knox Street, Abbeyquarter North, Sligo, (087) 177 2732.
- **Fáilte Ireland**, 85-95 Amiens Street, Dublin 1, www.failteireland.ie, customersupport@failteireland.ie, 1800 242473.
- **FarmDrop**, Unit A502, The Biscuit Factory, 100 Drummond Road, London SE1 4DG, www.farmdrop.com, hello@farmdrop.com, (0203) 770 9300.
- **Farmview Dairies**, 75a Lisnabreeny Road, Belfast BT6 9SR, www.farmviewdairies.net, (028) 9044 8553.
- **Featherbed Farm Luxury Ice Cream**, Featherbed Lane, Oylegate, Co. Wexford, www.featherbedfarm.ie, info@featherbedfarm.ie, (053) 917 7581.
- **Federation of Irish Beekeepers' Associations**, c/o Michael Gleeson (Hon. Sec.), Ballinakill, Enfield, Co. Meath, www.irishbeekeeping.ie, mgglee@eircom.net, (046) 954 1433.
- **Ferbane Food Campus, Ferbane, Co. Offaly**, www.ferbanefoodcampus.ie, (0906) 453926.
- **Fivemiletown Creamery**, 14 Ballylurgan Road, Fivemiletown, Co. Tyrone BT75 0RX, www.fivemiletowncheese.com, enquiries@dalefarm.co.uk, (028) 9037 2200.
- **Fiverr.com.**
- **FixItFood Ltd.**, Drumloona, Carrigallen, Co. Leitrim, www.fixitfood.com, (087) 310 4580.
- **Food Business Incubation Centre**, Loughry Campus, Cookstown, Co. Tyrone, www.cafre.ac.uk.
- **Food Flow Training**, Kinturk, Ballyheane, Co. Mayo, www.foodflow.ie, joe@foodflow.ie, (094) 903 0537.
- **Food Industry Training Unit**, College of Science, Engineering and Food Science, University College Cork, www.ucc.ie/fitu, m.mccarthybuckley@ucc.ie, (021) 490 3363.
- **Food Safety Authority of Ireland**, Abbey Court, Lower Abbey Street, Dublin 1, www.fsai.ie, info@fsai.ie, Advice line 1890 336677.

- **Food Standards Agency Northern Ireland**, 10c Clarendon Road, Belfast BT1 3BG, www.food.gov.uk/northern-ireland, (028) 9041 7700.
- **Food Standards Scotland**, 4th floor, Pilgrim House, Aberdeen, AB11 5RL, www.foodstandards.gov.scot.
- **Food Works**, www.foodworksireland.com, info@foodworksireland.com, (01) 668 5155.
- **FoodNI, Taste of Ulster**, Belfast Mills, 71-75 Percy Street, Belfast BT13 2HW, www.nigoodfood.com, info@nigoodfood.com, (028) 9024 9449.
- **Fullwood Ltd**, Grange Road, Ellesmere, Shropshire SY12 9DF, www.fullwood.com, sales@fullwood.com, (01691) 627391.
- **Fuschia Brands**, West Cork Technology Park, Clonakilty, Co. Cork, www.westcorkaplaceapart.com, info@westcorkaplaceapart.com, (023) 883 4035.
- **G&S Services Bakery Equipment Ltd.**, Unit 3, Hazelbank Mill, Gilford, Craigavon, Co. Armagh BT63 6DS, www.gandsbakeryequipment.co.uk, gandsservices@aol.com, (028) 4066 0492.
- **Gino's Gelatos**, Unit A7, Network Enterprise Park, Kilcoole, Co. Wicklow, www.ginosgelato.com, info@ginosgelato.com, (01) 201 1705.
- **Glastry Farm Ice Cream**, 43 Manse Road, Kirkubbin, Newtownards, Co. Down BT22 1DR, www.glastryfarm.com, (028) 4273 8671.
- **Glenfin Free Range Duck Eggs**, Drumbenagh, Tydavnet, Co. Monaghan, www.glenfinfarm.ie, info@glenfinfarm.ie, (086) 171 4240.
- **Glenilen Farm**, Drimoleague, Co. Cork, www.glenilenfarm.com, val@glenilenfarm.com, (028) 31179.
- **Glenisk Organic Dairy**, Killeigh, Co. Offaly, www.glenisk.com, info@glenisk.com, (057) 934 4000.
- **Glyde Farm Produce**, Mansfieldstown, Castlebellingham, Co. Louth, glydefarm@eircom.net, (042) 937 2343.
- **Goat Nutrition Ltd.**, Units B&C, Smarsden Business Estate, Monks Hill, Smarsden, Ashford, Kent TN2 8QL, www.gnltd.co.uk, (01233) 770780.
- **Good Food Ireland**, Ballykelly House, Drinagh, Co. Wexford, www.goodfoodireland.ie, info@goodfoodireland.ie, (053) 915 8693.
- **Goodness Grains**, Unit 2, Templemichael Business Park, Ballinalee Road, Longford, www.goodnessgrains.com, info@goodnessgrains.com, (043) 333 6698.

- **Graze, Nature Delivered Ltd.**, Palm Court, 4 Heron Square, Richmond, Surrey TW9 1EW, www.graze.com.
- **Great Taste Awards**, Guild of Fine Food, Guild House, 23b Kingsmead Business Park, Shaftesbury Road, Gillingham, SP8 5FB, www.finefoodworld.co.uk, info@finefoodworld.co.uk, (01747) 825 200.
- **Grow It Yourself** (GIY), www.giyinternational.org, info@giyireland.com, (051) 302191.
- **Gumtree.ie / Gumtree.co.uk.**
- **Happy Days Ice Cream**, Unit 10, Cherrywood, Courthouse Industrial Estate, Little Island, Cork, www.happydaysicecream.ie, danhappydaysicecream@gmail.com, (087) 610 0792.
- **Health Service Executive / Environmental Health Officers**, Oak House, Millennium Park, Naas, Co. Kildare, www.hse.ie/eng/services/list/1/environ/Contact.html, (045) 880400.
- **HelloFresh**, Grocery Delivery E-Services Inc., 40 West 25th Street, 7th Floor, New York, NY10010, www.hellofresh.com, hello@hellofresh.com.
- **Hillcrest Home Bakery**, Cloonamna, Kilmovee, Ballaghaderreen, Co. Mayo, (094) 964 9522.
- **Honest Bakery**, Unit 7 & 8, Enterprise Centre, Racecourse Road, Roscommon, www.honestbakery.ie, info@honestbakery.ie, (090) 662 5940.
- **Horgan's Delicatessen Ltd.**, Mitchelstown Co. Cork, www.horgans.com, enquiries@horgans.com, (025) 41200.
- **Improper Butter**, www.improperbutter.com, hey@improperbutter.com.
- **Independent Irish Health Foods Ltd.**, Unit 12, Ballyvourney Industrial Estate, Ballyvourney, Co. Cork, www.iihealthfoods.com, (026) 65750.
- **IndieFude**, Independent Food Co., The Courtyard, 5a High Street, Comber BT23 5HJ, www.indiefude.com, hello@indiefude.com, (07510) 728109.
- **Innovation Vouchers (Enterprise Ireland)**, www.innovationvouchers.ie.
- **Intellectual Property Office (UK)**, Concept House, Cardiff Road, Newport, South Wales NP10 8QQ, ipo.gov.uk, enquiries@ipo.gov.uk, (01633) 814000.

- **International Natural Sausage Casing Association**, 136 Gala El Dessouky Street, #505, Waboor El Maya, Alexandria, Egypt, www.insca.org, (122) 317 3612.
- **InterTradeIreland**, Old Gasworks Business Park, Kilmorey Street, Newry, Co. Down BT34 2DE, www.intertradeireland.com, info@intertradeireland.com, (028) 3083 4164.
- **InvestNI**, Bedford Square, Bedford Street, Belfast BT2 7ES, www.investni.com, (028) 9069 8000.
- **Irish Casing Company Ltd**, Spollanstown, Tullamore, Co. Offaly, www.irishcasings.com, info@irishcasings.com, (057) 932 1714.
- **Irish Countrywomen's Association**, 58 Merrion Road, Dublin 4, www.ica.ie, office@ica.ie, (01) 668 0002.
- **Irish Farmers Association**, Irish Farm Centre, Bluebell, Dublin 12, www.ifa.ie, postmaster@ifa.ie, (01) 450 0266.
- **Irish Food Co-op**, Kilkenny, www.irishfoodcoop.com, info@irishfoodcoop.com, (056) 780 0577.
- **Irish Food Writers Guild**, www.irishfoodwritersguild.ie.
- **Irish Fowl**, www.irishfowl.com.
- **Irish Organic Farmers and Growers Association**, Unit 16A, Inish Carrig, Golden Island, Athlone, Co. Westmeath, www.iofga.org, info@iofga.org, (0906) 43680.
- **Irish Organisation Market and Street Traders (IOMST)**, Bushfield Square, Philipsburgh Avenue, Fairview, Dublin 3, www.iomst.ie, info@iomst.ie, (01) 836 0952.
- **Irish Village Markets Ltd.**, 7 Windsor Place, Lanesville, Dun Laoire, Co. Dublin, www.irishvillagemarkets.ie, info@irishvillagemarkets.ie, (01) 284 1197.
- **Irish Yogurts**, Clonakilty, West Cork, www.irish-yogurts.ie, (023) 883 4745.
- **Irish-Poultry.com**.
- *Jab, Jab, Jab, Right Hook*, book by Gary Vaynerchuk, Harper Business, about social media marketing strategies.
- **Jack and Eddie's Sausages**, Westport, Co. Mayo, www.jackandeddies.com, info@jackandeddies.com, (087) 234 9945.

- **James McGeough Butchers**, Camp Street, Oughterard, Co. Galway, www.connemarafinefoods.ie, connemarafinefoods@eircom.net, (091) 552 351.
- **James Whelan Butchers**, Oakville Shopping Centre, Clonmel, Co. Tipperary, www.jameswhelanbutchers.com, (052) 618 2477.
- **Jongia**, PO Box 284, 8901 BB Leeuwarden, The Netherlands, www.jongia.com, info@jongia.com, (0582) 139715.
- **Kennedy Food Technology**, louiseakennedy@gmail.com, (086) 170 6939.
- **Killeen Farmhouse Cheese,** Loughanroe East, Ballyshrule, Ballinasloe, Co. Galway, www.killeencheese.ie, killeen.cheese@gmail.com, (0909) 741319.
- **Killowen Farm**, Courtnacuddy, Co. Wexford, www.killowen.ie, pauline@killowen.ie, (053) 924 4819.
- **Knockanore Farmhouse Cheese Co. Ltd.**, Knockanore, Co. Waterford, www.knockanorecheese.com, eamon@knockanorecheese.com, (024) 97275.
- **Knockdrinna Farmhouse Cheese**, Stoneyford, Co. Kilkenny, www.knockdrinna.com, orders@knockdrinna.com, (056) 772 8446.
- **Kookee**, Dundalk, Co. Louth, www.kookee.ie, info@kookee.ie.
- **Larder360**, Unit 16, Westlink Commercial Park, Oranmore, Co. Galway, www.larder360.com, info@larder360.com, (091) 792899.
- **LEADER / Rural Development Partnership Companies**, www.nationalruralnetwork.ie / www.leader-programme.co.uk.
- **Leatherhead Food Research**, Randalls Road, Leatherhead, Surrey KT22 7RY, www.leatherheadfood.com, help@leatherheadfood.com, (01372) 376761.
- **Limerick Food Centre**, Raheen, Limerick.
- **Linnalla Ice Cream**, New Quay, The Burren, Co. Clare, www.linnallaicecream.ie, info@linnallaicecream.ie, (065) 707 8167.
- **Local Enterprise Offices**, www.localenterprise.ie.
- **London Farmers' Markets**, 11 O'Donnell Court, Brunswick Centre, London WC1N 1NY, www.lfm.org.uk, info@lfm.co.uk, (0207) 833 0338.
- **Love Irish Food**, www.loveirishfood.ie.

- **M&K Meats Ltd.**, Unit 14 Block G, Greenogue Business Park, Rathcoole, Co. Dublin, www.mkmeats.eu, info@mkmeats.eu, (01) 458 7942.
- **MacEoin Poultry Supplies Ltd.**, Ballydavid, Co. Kerry, www.maceoinltd.com, (087) 207 7019.
- **Macroom Buffalo Cheese**, Kilnamartyra Post Office, Clonclud, Macroom, Co. Cork, www.macroombuffalocheese.com, (026) 41907.
- **Macs BBQ**, Unit 3A Rosevear Road Industrial Estate, Bugle, Cornwall, www.macsbbq.co.uk (01726) 851495.
- **Mallow Mia**, Ardee, Newtowncunningham, Co. Donegal, www.mallowmia.com, hello@mallowmia.com, (086) 273 6181.
- *Manufacturing Yogurt and Fermented Milks*, book by RC Chandan, Wiley-Blackwell.
- **Markets Alive Support Team Ltd. (MAST)**, Clarinda Mews, 23 Clarinda Park West, Dun Laoire, Co. Dublin, www.mast.ie, info@mast.ie, (01) 230 0788.
- **Martin Food Equipment**, Dundalk, www.martinfoodequip.com, info@martinfoodequip.com, 1850 30 36 36.
- **Mash Direct Ltd.**, 81 Ballyrainey Road, Comber, Co. Down BT23 5JU, www.mashdirect.com, (028) 9187 8316.
- **McDonnell's Ltd.**, 19-20 Blackhall Street, Dublin 7, www.mcdonnells.ie, sales@mcdonnells.ie / info@mcdonnells.ie.
- **McGrath Bakery Services Ltd.**, 35a Donacloney Road, Dromore BT25 1JR, www.mbs-ltd.org, info@mbs-ltd.org, (028) 3888 1200.
- *Microbiology and Technology of Fermented Foods*, book by RW Hutkins.
- **MicroFinance Ireland**, 13 Richview Office Park, Clonskea Road, Dublin 14, www.microfinanceireland.ie, info@microfinanceireland.ie, (01) 260 1007.
- **Mileeven Fine Foods**, Owning Hill, Piltown, Co. Kilkenny, www.mileeven.com, admin@mileeven.com, (051) 643368.
- **Milk Development Council** – see DairyCo.
- **Moorlands Cheesemakers Ltd.**, Lorien House, South Street, Castle Cary, Somerset BA7 7ES, www.cheesemaking.co.uk, info@cheesemaking.co.uk, (01963) 350634.

- **Morelli Ice Cream Ltd.**, Unit 27, Sperrin Business Park, Coleraine, Co. Londonderry BT52 2DH, www.morellisices.com, (028) 7025 7155.
- **Moy Valley Resources IRD**, Greenhills Enterprise Centre, Bunree Road, Ballina, Co. Mayo, www.moyvalley.ie, info@moyvalley.ie, (096) 70905.
- **Murphy's Ice Cream**, Strand Street, Dingle, Co. Kerry, www.murphysicecream.ie, (066) 915 2644.
- **Musgrave Food Services**, Musgrave Retailer Services, St. Margaret's Road, Ballymun, Dublin 11, foodservices.musgrave.ie, helpdesk2@musgrave.ie, (1890) 886 800.
- **Namecheck.com.**
- **National Dairy Council**, Innovation House, 3 Arkle Road, Sandyford Industrial Estate, Dublin 18, www.ndc.ie, info@ndc.ie, (01) 290 2451.
- **National Organic Training Skillnet** (NOTS), The Enterprise Centre, Hill Road, Drumshanbo, Co. Leitrim, www.nots.ie, info@nots.ie, (071) 964 0688 / (086) 172 8442.
- **National Ploughing Association**, Fallaghmore, Athy, Co. Kildare, www.npa.ie, info@npa.ie, (059) 862 5125.
- **Newmarket Kitchen**, Unit 3, Atlas Court, IDA Business Park, Southern Cross Road, Bray, Co. Wicklow, www.newmarketkitchen.ie, hello@newmarketkitchencom.
- **Nisbets Next Day Catering Equipment**, North Link Business Park, Old Mallow Road, Cork, www.nisbets.ie, sales@nisbets.ie, (021) 494 6777.
- **North Tipperary Food Works**, Rearcross, Co. Tipperary, www.northtippfoodworks.ie, northtippfoodworks@gmail.com, (067) 33086.
- **Nutgrove Enterprise Park**, Nutgrove Way, Rathfarnham, Dublin 14, www.nutgrove-enterprisepark.ie, info@dlrceb.ie, (01) 494 8400.
- **Old McDonald's Farm & Feed Store**, Co. Carlow, www.oldmcdonald.ie, info@oldmcdonald.ie, (059) 917 9548 / (087) 279 7705.
- **Old Smokehouse Foods & Equipment**, Cookequip Ltd., Unit 4, Sumner Place, Addlestone, Surrey KT15 1QD, www.the-old-smokehouse.co.uk, sales@cookequip.co.uk, (01932) 841171.

- *On-farm Processing: A Beginner's Guide*, published by the Milk Development Council.
- *On-farm Small-scale Cheese-making: A Beginner's Guide*, available from DairyCo.
- **Organic Trust Ltd.**, Vernon House, 2 Vernon Avenue, Clontarf, Dublin 3, www.organic-trust.org, organic@iol.ie, (01) 853 0271.
- **Paganini Ice Cream**, Kerlogue Industrial Centre, Rosslare Road, Wexford, www.paganini.ie, info@paganini.ie, (053) 914 7222.
- **Pallas Foods**, Newcastle West, Co. Limerick, www.pallasfoods.eu, info@pallasfoods.eu, (069) 20200.
- **Parkview Farm**, Tourlestrane, Co. Sligo, www.parkviewduckfarm.com, (087) 291 2664.
- **Pat O'Doherty**, Belmore Street, Enniskillen, Co. Fermanagh, www.blackbacon.com, p@blackbacon.com, (028) 6632 2152.
- **Patents Office**, Government Buildings, Hebron Road, Kilkenny, www.patentsoffice.ie, patlib@patentsoffice.ie, (056) 772 0111.
- **Poacher's Premium Beverages**, www.poacherswell.com, info@poacherswell.com.
- **Poultry Ireland**, www.poultry.ie.
- *Practical Poultry*, www.practicalpoultry.co.uk.
- **Pure Bred**, Gallagher's Bakery, Ardara, Co. Donegal, www.purebred.co.uk, info@purebred.co.uk, (074) 953 7500.
- **Quality Food Awards**, Metropolis Business Publishing, 6th Floor, Davis House, 2 Robert Street, Croydon CR0 1QQ, www.qualityfoodawards.com.
- *Quick Win Digital Marketing*, book / ebook by Annmarie Hanlon and Joanna Akins, Oak Tree Press (www.successstore.com).
- *Quick Win Marketing*, book / ebook by Annmarie Hanlon, Oak Tree Press (www.successstore.com).
- *Quick Win Social Media Marketing*, book / ebook by Annmarie Hanlon, Oak Tree Press (www.successstore.com).
- **Quickcrop**, Unit 4, Ballymote Industrial Estate, Ballymote, Co. Sligo, www.quickcrop.ie, info@quickcrop.ie, (01) 524 0884.
- **Quinn's Quacks**, Classaroe, Ballyhaunis, Co. Mayo, (086) 395 7059.

- **Rademaker BV**, Plantjinweg 23, PO Box 416, 4100 AK Culemborg, The Netherlands, www.rademaker.com, office@rademaker.com, (0345) 543 543.
- **Rafferty's Fine Foods**, Blackrock, Dundalk, Co. Louth, www.raffertysfinefoods.ie, info@raffertysfinefoods.ie, (087) 287 1080.
- **Rainbow Free Range Poultry**, Derrydonnell Mor, Athenry, Co. Galway, www.freerangepoultry.ie, tara@freerangepoultry.ie, (087) 919 9699.
- **Richmount Cordial Company**, Carrickboy, Co. Longford, www.richmountcordials.ie, martina@richmountcordials.ie, (087) 831 6688 / (087) 646 4757.
- **Robot Coupe (UK) Ltd.**, 2 Fleming Way, Isleworth TW7 6EU, www.robotcoupe.co.uk, sales@robotcoupe.co.uk, (0208) 232 1800.
- **Rosaleen's Kitchen**, Coralstown, Mullingar, Co. Westmeath, www.facebook.com / pg / rosaleenskitchens, (087) 237 4268.
- **Rossmore Farmhouse Ice Cream**, Erril, Rathdowney, Co. Laois, www.rossmorefarm.ie, rossmoreicecream@gmail.com, (0505) 44292.
- **RSS Ltd.**, Hereford, Station Approach, Hereford, HR1 1BB, www.rsshereford.co.uk, sales@rsshereford.co.uk, (01432) 276777.
- **Rural Development Partnerships / LEADER Companies**, www.nationalruralnetwork.ie / www.leader-programme.co.uk.
- **SafeFood**, 7 Eastgate Avenue, Eastgate, Little Island, Cork, www.safefood.eu, (021) 230 4100.
- **Scobie & Junor (Dublin) Ltd.**, Unit D2, M7 Business Park, Newhall Interchange, Naas, Co. Kildare, www.scobiesdirect.com, info@scobiesdirect.com, (045) 899 177.
- **Scobie Bakery**, Scobie McIntosh Ltd, Oakwell Business Centre, Dark Lane, West Yorkshire WF14 9LW, www.scobiebakery.com, (01924) 432940.
- **Sea Fisheries Protection Authority**, Park Road, Clogheen, Clonakilty, Co. Cork, www.sfpa.ie, sfpa_info@sfpa.ie, (023) 885 9300.
- **Servequip**, Suite 8, The Swift Centre, 41 Imperial Way, Croydon, Surrey CR0 4RL, www.servequip.co.uk, info@servequip.co.uk, (0208) 686 8855.
- **Silver Pail Dairy**, Dublin Road, Fermoy, Co. Cork, www.silverpail.com, info@silverpail.com, (025) 31466.

- **Simply Fit Food**, Ardee Business Park, Broadlough, Ardee, Co. Louth, www.simplyfitfood.com.
- **Skillnets**, www.skillnets.ie.
- **Slow Food Ireland**, www.slowfoodireland.com.
- **Small Firms Association**, 84-86 Lower Baggot Street, Dublin 2, www.sfa.ie, info@sfa.ie, (01) 605 1500.
- **Smallholding Ireland**, www.smallholding.ie.
- **Smoky Jo's Cooking School**, Castle Court, Shap, Penrith, Cumbria CA10 3LG, www.smokyjos.co.uk, info@smokyjos.co.uk, (01931) 716638.
- **Society of Dairy Technology**, Larnick Park, Higher Larrick, Trebullet, Launceston, Cornwall PL15 9QH, www.sdt.org, execdirector@sdt.org, (0845) 528 0418.
- **Somerset Local Food Direct**, Unit 1, Thomas Way, Glastonbury, BA6 9LU, www.localfooddirect.co.uk, mail@localfooddirect.co.uk, (01458) 830801.
- **SPADE Enterprise Centre**, St. Paul's Church, North King Street, Dublin 7, (01) 617 4830, contact Susan Richardson, Centre Manager.
- **Specialist Cheesemakers Association**, 17 Clerkenwell Green, London EC1R 0DP, www.specialistcheesemakers.co.uk, info@specialistcheesemakers.co.uk, (0207) 608 1645.
- **Speciality & Fine Food Fair**, Fresh Montgomery, www.specialtyandfinefoodfair.co.uk, info@montex.co.uk, (0207) 886 3000.
- **St. Angela's College**, Lough Gill, Sligo, stangelas.nuigalway.ie, admin@stangelas.nuigalway.ie, (071) 914 3580.
- *Starting a Business in Ireland*, 7th edition, book / ebook by Brian O'Kane, Oak Tree Press (www.successstore.com).
- *Starting Your Own Business: A Workbook*, 4th edition, book by Ron Immink and Brian O'Kane, Oak Tree Press (www.successstore.com).
- **Stratton Sales & Service Inc.**, 1215 South Swaner Road, Salt Lake City, Utah 84104, USA, www.strattonsales.com, info@strattonsales.com, (801) 973 4041.
- **Straw Chip**, Ballycullane, Athy, Co. Kildare, (059) 863 1623.
- **Sugarcraft.ie**, 64A Georges Street Upper, Dun Laoire, Co. Dublin, www.sugarcraft.ie, info@sugarcraft.ie, (01) 280 1870.
- **SupportingSMEs.ie**.

- **Sweet Beat Café**, Bridge Street, Sligo, www.sweetbeat.ie, hello@sweetbeat.ie, (071) 913 8795.
- **Taste 4 Success Skillnet**, PO Box 113, Rathowen, Co. Westmeath, www.taste4success.ie, info@taste4success.ie, (043) 668 5289.
- **TASTE Council**, www.tastecouncilofireland.com.
- **Taste of Scotland**, www.taste-of-scotland.com, info@taste-of-scotland.com.
- **Teagasc (HQ)**, Oak Park, Carlow, www.teagasc.ie, (059) 917 0200.
- **Teagasc**, Ashtown, Dublin 15, www.teagasc.ie, (01) 805 9500.
- **Teagasc**, Moorepark Food Research Centre, Fermoy, www.teagasc.ie, niamh.obrien@teagasc.ie, (025) 42222.
- **Terenure Enterprise Centre**, Terenure, Dublin 6W, www.terenure-enterprise.ie, mhannan@terenure-enterprise.ie, (01) 490 3237.
- **The Cheese Hub**, Drumshambo, Co. Leitrim, www.thecheesehub.ie, info@thecheesehub.ie, (086) 172 8442 / (087) 273 7538.
- **The Cheese Web**, Eclectic Events Ltd., Old Woolman's House, Hastings Hill, Churchill, Oxfordshire OX7 6NA, www.thecheeseweb.com, cheese@thecheeseweb.com, (01608) 659325.
- *The Composition of Foods*, book by McCance and Widdowson, Royal Society of Chemistry.
- **The Cultured Club**, www.theculturedclub.com.
- **The Food Hub**, Carrick Road, Drumshanbo, Co. Leitrim, www.thefoodhub.com, info@thefoodhub.com, (071) 964 1848.
- **The Food Technology Centre**, St. Angela's College, Lough Gill, Sligo, www.thefoodtechnologycentre.ie, info@thefoodtechnologycentre, (071) 915 0734.
- **The Foods of Athenry**, Oldcastle, Kilconieron, Athenry, Co. Galway, www.foodsofathenry.ie, info@foodsofathenry.ie, (091) 848152.
- **The Ice Cream Alliance**, 3 Melbourne Court, off Island No. One, Derwent Parade, Pride Park, Derby DE24 8LZ, www.ice-cream.org, info@ice-cream.org, (01332) 203333.
- **The Knead for Bread**, www.thekneadforbread.com.
- **The Organic Centre**, Rossinver, Co. Leitrim, www.theorganiccentre.ie, info@theorganiccentre.ie, (071) 985 4338.
- *The Sausage Book* by Paul Peacock, Kitchen Newbie.

- **The School of Food**, Dublin Road, Thomastown, Co. Kilkenny, www.schooloffood.ie, info@schooloffood.ie, (056) 775 4397.
- **The Stallholders Club**, Pierpoint International Trading Ltd., Unit 25A, 25Floor, Wing Hing Commercial Building, 139 Wing Lok Street, Sheun Wang, Hong Kong, www.stallholders.org.
- **Tickety-Moo**, 38 Tully Road, Oghill, Irvinestown, Enniskillen, Co. Fermanagh.
- **Tipperary Organic Ice Cream**, c/o The Chocolate Garden, Tullow, Co. Carlow, www.tipperaryorganic.ie, info@tipperaryorganic.ie, (059) 648 1999.
- **Traditional Cheese Company**, Unit 244, Holly Road, Western Industrial Estate, Dublin 12, www.traditionalcheese.ie, info@traditionalcheese.ie, (01) 450 9494.
- **Truly Irish Country Foods Ltd.**, Newcastle West, Co. Limerick, www.trulyirish.ie, (069) 78334.
- **Údarás na Gaeltachta**, Na Forbacha, Co. na Gaillimhe, www.udaras.ie, eolas@udaras.ie, (091) 503100.
- **Ummera Smoked Products Ltd.**, Timoleague, Co. Cork, www.ummera.com, info@ummera.com, (023) 884 6644.
- **Valentia Island Farmhouse Dairy**, Valentia, Co. Kerry, www.valentiadairy.com, valentiaicecream@eircom.net, (066) 947 6864.
- **Velvet Cloud**, Rockfield Dairy, Rockfield, Claremorris, Co. Mayo, www.velvetcloud.ie, michael@rockfielddairy.com / aisling@rockfielddairy.com, (087) 639 0841 / (087) 988 1583.
- **West Cork Pies**, Unit 4, Coronea Enterprise Centre, Skibbereen, Co. Cork, www.westcorkpies.com, (028) 51824.
- **Westport Grove Jams and Chutneys**, Westport, Co. Mayo, absfcasey@eircom.net, (087) 237 2479, contact Sean Casey.
- **Wholefoods Wholesale Ltd.**, www.wholefoods.ie.
- **Woodlands Dairy**, Sunrise Business Park, Blandford Forum, Dorset DT11 8ST, www.woodlandsdairy.co.uk, sales@woodlandsdairy.co.uk, (0845) 467 9894.
- **Wyldsson Ltd.**, Tallaght Business Centre, Whitestown Business Park, Tallaght, Dublin 24, www.wyldsson.com, hello@wyldsson.com, (01) 452 4042.
- **Yorkshire Pantry**, Unit 8, Blackwood Hall Business Park, Cornelius Causeway, North Duffield, Selby, North Yorkshire YO8 5DD,

www.theyorkshirepantry.com, info@ theyorkshirepantry.com,
(0113) 328 0823.

ABOUT THE AUTHOR

OONAGH MONAHAN has worked in, for and with the food industry for over 20 years, doing everything ranging from waitressing and dishwashing for the hospitality sector, working in the fast food industry, to food technologist and quality manager in the poultry and bakery sectors, and finally onto food business consultancy. She has a Graduate Diploma in Food Science and Technology from the Dublin Institute of Technology and a Master of Engineering Science degree by research thesis from the Department of Agricultural and Food Engineering at UCD. For this research, Oonagh won a scholarship sponsored by H.J. Heinz to study salad cream in great detail! In addition, Oonagh has a Diploma in Training and Education from NUI Galway and has a Post Graduate Diploma in Business & Management from the William J. Clinton Leadership Institute at Queen's University Belfast.

Oonagh is a Fellow of the Institute of Food Science and Technology (UK), a Fellow of the Institute of Food Science and Technology of Ireland, a Certified Management Consultant and a member of the Institute of Management Consultants and Advisors.

Her experience includes roles as Food Technologist and Quality Control Manager with Manor Bakeries Ltd. (Mr. Kipling cakes) in England and Quality Assurance Manager with Kerry Foods (Grove Turkeys) in Co. Monaghan. Oonagh subsequently took a position as General Manager of the Food Technology Centre at St Angela's College, Sligo, where she was responsible for business development of the centre, as well as forming and managing collaborative food innovation projects between academia and client food companies. Oonagh has also lectured in food New Product Development and in EU and Irish Food legislation.

In January 2008, Oonagh set up Alpha Omega Consultants (**www.alphaomega.ie**), where she uses her extensive experience to devise, deliver, facilitate and manage support programmes for the food sector. She is a mentor with Enterprise Ireland, several Local Enterprise Offices and Rural Development Companies for new food start-up companies. She also delivers Start Your Own Food Business courses across the country and has been a trainer and facilitator for the Bord Bia / SuperValu Food Academy programme since 2013. Oonagh was a founder of the Harvest Feast Food Festival in Leitrim and also has been involved with the So Sligo Food Festival and Sligo Food Trail. Oonagh has the very difficult task of being one of the judges for the Irish Quality Food Awards – it's not easy!

Oonagh is a keen home cook and has attended several courses at the Neven Maguire, Ballymaloe and Belle Isle cookery schools. She has a real interest in the preparation, presentation and service of good food, using quality ingredients, local and seasonal where possible, whether fine dining, gastro pub or at home. However, she's not precious about it and recognises the needs of the industry and is pragmatic in her approach. Oonagh always tries to educate consumers – read the labels, people! She has travelled in the UK, USA, France, Holland, Italy, Spain, Malaysia, Canada, Singapore, Croatia and Hungary, as well as extensive travelling across the island of Ireland, eating her way around (!), always interested in trying new foods. Places to eat while on the road or on holiday take top priority!

You can follow Oonagh on Twitter **@oonagheats** and **@OMAlphaOmega**, on LinkedIn, her website **www.alphaomega.ie**, her blog **oonagheats.com** and find her on **Facebook.com/MoneyForJamEssentialGuide** and **/oonagheats** and **/OMAlphaOmegaConsultants**.

OAK TREE PRESS

Oak Tree Press develops and delivers information, advice and resources for entrepreneurs and managers. It is Ireland's leading business book publisher, with an unrivalled reputation for quality titles across business, management, HR, law, marketing and enterprise topics. NuBooks is its ebook-only imprint, publishing short, focused ebooks for busy entrepreneurs and managers.

In addition, through its founder and managing director, Brian O'Kane, Oak Tree Press occupies a unique position in start-up and small business support in Ireland through its standard-setting titles, as well as training courses, mentoring and advisory services.

Oak Tree Press is comfortable across a range of communication media – print, web and training, focusing always on the effective communication of business information.

OAK TREE PRESS

33 Rochestown Rise, Rochestown, Cork T12EVT0, Ireland.
T: + 353 086 244 1633 / 086 330 7694.
E: info@oaktreepress.com
W: www.oaktreepress.com / www.SuccessStore.com.